Accounting Thought and Education:

SIX ENGLISH PIONEERS

J. KITCHEN

(Professor of Accounting in the University of Hull)

and

R. H. PARKER

(Professor of Accountancy in the University of Exeter)

With a Foreword by Douglas Morpeth

The Institute of Chartered Accountants
in England and Wales
Chartered Accountants' Hall, Moorgate Place,
London, EC2P 2BJ
1980

This book is published by the Technical and Research Committee of the Institute of Chartered Accountants in England and Wales, but does not necessarily share the views expressed, which are those of the authors alone.

ISBN 0 85291 267 6

The four Fred May cartoons are reproduced from *The Accountant* by courtesy of Gee & Co. (Publishers) Ltd., and the cover photograph by permission of the *Sunday Times*.

Printed by The Institute of Chartered Accountants in England and Wales

FOREWORD

Members of the English Institute will rightly spend 1980 proud of the achievement of their Institute in reaching the age of 100 years in very good heart and shape to withstand the rigours and challenges of the next hundred. During the first hundred years the Institute has grown in size and stature; its voice, now joined with the other CCAB bodies, is listened to with respect on accounting, legal, financial, auditing and taxation matters not only in the UK but around the world.

It has over the years raised the whole standard of education and training for membership, and has recently introduced continuing professional education to keep members up to date once qualified. There is an immense courses and publications programme to achieve this. There is a new disciplinary procedure to punish those who fail to respond and who produce poor professional work. The Accounting Standards Committee has been established to produce accounting standards, and an Auditing Practices Committee to produce auditing standards. Much more is being spent on research and the Institute has proved not unwilling to enter difficult frontier areas such as seeking a conceptual framework to reporting, publishing a Corporate Report discussing the future communication role, and seeking with success after a difficult but determined struggle to introduce a method of accounting to cope with the effect of changing price levels.

Members have acquired the new skills required to provide new services as demanded by the public and have been successful in most activities where accounting, financial and management abilities are required. Many accounting firms have even in the last decade returned successfully to insolvency work, from which members in the last century tried to escape.

All this, however, has not happened by accident. It has happened because some individual members have devoted time, energy and skill, not only towards their own interests, but towards improving the profession to which they belonged.

It is particularly apt that as we enjoy the success of our Institute in its one hundredth year, Professors Kitchen and Parker should publish this book, covering the lives and contribution of six English pioneers, so that we are reminded that we owe much to men whom we have perhaps lost sight of and whose contributions we have forgotten. Of course, the authors could have picked others than the six chosen, but it is perhaps understandable that they chose men whose contribution was as thinkers and writers, although, like all members of our profession, they were doers as well.

The era in which some of them developed their careers was one in which accounting was only just beginning to be established - it could not be said that proper books of account were kept in the way we think today of the meaning of that term; secret reserves were considered in a favourable light; there was no uniformity in the way companies presented their annual accounts. Indeed, Edwin Guthrie's (1841-1904) first published article was entitled 'The Want of Uniformity in the Modes of Stating Accounts, the Frequency of Inconsistency between the Title and Subject Matter of Published Accounts, and the Employment of Non-correlative Terms in Accounts'. He argued for consistency of treatment - one of the four fundamental concepts underlying accounts referred to in SSAP 2. Again, it was Francis Pixley (1852-1933) who stressed the need for all companies to have an audit, who wrote the first text book on auditing and who laid great stress on the prudence and going concern concepts.

The authors have rightly put some emphasis on those practising accountants whose contribution was perhaps largely in the auditing field, including Cutforth and Dicksee, who devoted much of their interest to the education of students. (Indeed, Dicksee was the first man to be appointed to a university chair in accounting.) They have however not forgotten the pioneering works of industrial accountants like John Manger Fells (1858-1925) whose book on Factory Accounts published in 1887 was the leading English work on costing until the First World War; and Frederic de Paula, the first non-practising accountant appointed to the English Institute Council, and a leading light in the development of the Recommendations on Accounting Principles. These represented the first major effort at achieving some consistency of treatment and presentation of accounts, were a landmark of the day, and the forerunner of today's accounting standards.

It is not the function of a foreword to explain what is in the book, but to encourage people to read and enjoy its contents. I believe that, as accountants today, we should know something of our predecessors and how their major contribution has helped lay the foundations for our present state in this year of our centenary, 1980.

This book gives a fascinating insight into the lives and work of six of these predecessors.

19 March 1980 Douglas S. Morpeth

PREFACE

We are grateful to the Research Sub-Committee of the Institute of Chartered Accountants in England and Wales for their grant which helped to finance the research needed for this book. Needless to say, neither the Sub-Committee nor the Institute are responsible for the facts reported and the views expressed.

We are grateful also for supplementary financial support kindly provided by Arthur Andersen & Co. and Clark Pixley. We are indebted to Mr. K.B. Brooker, BA (Hull), now a Lecturer in the Department of Adult Education at the University of Leicester, for valuable research assistance in connection with genealogical, census, and other data; and we offer our sincere thanks to all those (within and without the accountancy profession) who have helped and guided us with information or recollections. We are particularly indebted to Mr. Douglas Morpeth for so generously undertaking to write a Foreword. In gratefully acknowledging the contributions to our task made by all these firms and individuals, we wish to stress that we alone are responsible for any errors of omission or commission.

No one interested in the history of accounting education and ideas in this country can work for long in the field without consciousness of the great benefits he derives from the collections of the Library of the Institute of Chartered Accountants in England and Wales and from its unfailingly helpful staff: we would like to record our thanks to them. We wish also to record our special obligation to Messrs. Gee & Co. and to successive Editors of The Accountant: without that rich source of historical material, upon which we have drawn so freely, this book could not have been written. We take this opportunity to commend the work of the Arno Press of New York, who in recent years have reprinted many of the books, lectures, and articles to which we refer and thereby made them widely available.

Finally, we would like to thank Mrs. Elvy Ibbotson and Mrs. Maureen M. Wilde for their patient and careful work on our drafts, and Mrs. Hilary Ireland for re-typing our material for reproduction.

J.K.
R.H.P.

CONTENTS

CHAPTER 1

INTRODUCTION

Practitioners of accounting have always needed the support of thinkers and writers in the education of new entrants and in the development of new ideas. This book is concerned with the lives and careers of six English pioneers in accounting thought and education:

Edwin Guthrie	1841-1904
Francis William Pixley	1852-1933
John Manger Fells	1858-1925
Lawrence Robert Dicksee	1864-1932
Arthur Edwin Cutforth	1881-1958
Frederic Rudolph Mackley de Paula	1882-1954

Edwin Guthrie had a substantial practice in Manchester before 1880, and was a member of the original Council of the Institute of Chartered Accountants in England and Wales (ICAEW) named in the Royal Charter. Francis Pixley and Arthur Cutforth were Presidents, each in his day, of the ICAEW. Lawrence Dicksee was the first man to be appointed to a University chair in Accounting. Frederic de Paula was the first non-practising accountant to be elected to the Council of the ICAEW. John Manger Fells was co-author of the most important work in the field of management accounting to be written in the nineteenth century; he became a member of the Council of the Society of Incorporated Accountants and Auditors and a Fellow of the then newly formed Institute of Cost and Works Accountants, now the Institute of Cost and Management Accountants.

Most members of most professions are necessarily doers rather than thinkers and writers. In that sense, our six pioneers were clearly not typical members of their profession, though they were typical in other ways. Pixley, Dicksee, Cutforth and de Paula all came from prosperous middle-class families as, until the Second World War, did a majority of the members of the ICAEW largely because of the premiums payable before entry to articles and the small (or non-existent) salaries commonly paid, to that time, during the years of articled clerkship. Guthrie and Fells came from humbler backgrounds. Fells was never a member of the ICAEW, and had Guthrie been aged 16 in 1880 (as Dicksee was) instead of being 39 and an established practitioner, it is unlikely that he would have been able to afford to become a chartered accountant. Like most accountants until very recently, none of them had a University first degree.

Guthrie, Pixley and Cutforth were outstandingly successful in public accountancy practice. de Paula also practised successfully until 1929, after which he became a leader among the growing number of professional accountants directly employed in industry. Dicksee was in public practice from the time he qualified (1886) until his death in 1932, but his affections lay mainly in his work as teacher and writer. Fells had preceded de Paula in the management accounting field.

The influence of these six men on the development of accounting ideas was very great, and was to persist throughout the period between the wars and into the 1950s and after.

Growth of the profession

The ICAEW was granted a royal charter in 1880. By 1885, the year in which the rival Society of Incorporated Accountants was formed, there were 1,371 English chartered accountants and 396 incorporated accountants. By the time Guthrie, the earliest of the pioneers, died in 1904, these numbers had increased to 3,117 and 2,068 respectively. In 1957, just before the death of the longest surviving of our six pioneers, and just before the merger of the chartered and incorporated accountants, there were 20,124 English chartered accountants, 11,335 incorporated accountants, 10,103 certified accountants and 5,758 cost and works accountants.

At the same time as the numbers increased, the scope of accountancy work expanded. This is reflected in the writings of our six pioneers which naturally concentrated on those matters of greatest interest in their times.

In a famous lecture given in 1921 ('Fifty-seven years in an accountant's office'), Ernest Cooper recorded how in the early days of the profession:

> An accountant was regarded as associated with and dependent upon insolvency ... I well remember that to be seen talking to or having your office entered by an accountant was to be avoided, particularly in the stressful times of 1866.

Cooper also remarked that 'Comparatively few large concerns, railways or banks, were audited by accountants'. This was soon to change.

Auditing

From the 1870s there was, for large organisations, a steady movement away from audits carried out by lay auditors (amateurs elected at general meetings by shareholders from among their own number) and towards the employment in their stead of professional accountants to undertake the audits and to report to shareholders on the annual accounts. The movement gained impetus following the bank failures of the 1860s and 1870s, and in the years leading up to and following the Railways Regulation Act of 1868. The 1879 companies legislation prescribed compulsory audits for banking companies. Joint stock companies registered under the Companies Acts were growing dramatically in numbers, and audits for all such companies were made compulsory in the companies legislation of 1900. A sharp increase in audit work for the generality of commercial and industrial businesses followed. Earlier, as indicated, the development had been in audit work for railways, banks and other financial undertakings, as well as for building societies, friendly and provident societies and similar organisations. The full title of Pixley's book, published in 1881 and the first of its kind, was _Auditors: their Duties and Responsibilities under the Joint-Stock Companies Acts and the Friendly Societies and Industrial and Provident Societies Acts_.

For the larger organisations, the necessity was for directors to be enabled to account to shareholders for the subscribed and loaned funds entrusted to their care; for shareholders to have assurance that actual or proposed dividends could be met out of income (paid out of profits and not out of capital); and for shareholders and others to have information to enable them to make some reasonable judgement as to the solvency of the organisation with which they were concerned.

Dicksee's _Auditing_, which appeared in 1892, very much lived up to its sub-title as 'A practical manual for auditors' and was aimed more directly than Pixley's at the generality of commercial and industrial organisations. Looking back fifty years or more, in an introductory article in the first issue of _Accounting Research_ (1948) de Paula commented:

> In practice, in those days, the majority of the new audits represented 'virgin soil', that is the books of account of that business had never before been examined by a professional accountant. In this way many strange systems of book-keeping came to light. It was by no means uncommon to find primitive records upon a single entry basis or alternatively most complicated double entry systems ...
>
> A great part of the work of practising accountants in those days was introducing double-entry systems and generally re-organising the book-keeping systems of their clients' businesses. The quintessence of modernity was to organise the ledgers upon a self-balancing system.

> The book-keeping staffs of those days were generally of poor quality, and ... it commonly fell to the auditor to balance the books and to prepare the annual accounts ...

Book-keeping systems were ill-supervised within the organisations concerned and fraud by employees was common.

Though they were by no means simply 'examination texts', Cutforth's Audits of 1906 and de Paula's Principles of Auditing of 1914 were aimed less at practitioners than had been Pixley's and Dicksee's works, and more at the growing number of students preparing for the ICAEW's half-yearly examinations. de Paula's book, in particular, was concerned (as its title suggested) to develop further the 'root principles' which formed the basis of all audit work.

It is indicative of the importance of auditing in the growth of the profession that four of our pioneers wrote important works on the subject, the first editions of which were published between 1881 and 1914.

Form and presentation of company accounts

As auditors, practising accountants inevitably became concerned with the form and presentation of company accounts. Guthrie's first published article (1882) was on the want of uniformity in accounts. British accountants have, however, typically taken more interest in what is disclosed (or not disclosed) in published accounts than in how it is disclosed.

The period before, and especially during, the First World War saw major changes in the size, organisation, and finance of businesses, especially of industrial undertakings and the technology and production methods on which they were based. At this time, secret or undisclosed inner reserves were widely employed. Their creation and use had become established practice, particularly in the last quarter of the 19th century, with the strong approval of shareholders and the capital market. Amalgamations and mergers of companies had become common, and the holding company group had begun to be important in Britain in the later years of the War. Groups of companies (parent or holding companies and subsidiaries) had for some time been established in the USA and were to become in Britain also the dominant form in organisation for large-scale business. Broadly speaking, accounting developments in Britain from the beginning of the 1920s to the companies legislation of 1947/48 followed from these main changes. During the intervening period, accountants and the business world came to grips with the problems caused by and the attitudes favouring secret reserves. At the same time there was a revolution in attitudes to the disclosure of financial information by companies and in the extent to which the Councils of the professional accountancy bodies were prepared to associate themselves and their members with statements outlining 'best practice' in company and group financial reporting. With these developments, de Paula was especially concerned.

Other accounting issues

There were, of course, many other controversial accounting issues. Only a few can be mentioned here. Much attention was given to depreciation. Guthrie's lecture of 1883 on the subject was the first one to be fully reported. During the careers of our six pioneers, the problem of changing price levels was not of practical concern in Britain save during and just after the two World Wars. It was briefly referred to by Fells and given rather more attention by de Paula but we do not deal with the subject in any detail in this book.

The local government reforms of the late 19th century engendered an interest in municipal accounts and audit. This was one or the subjects on which Guthrie, Chairman of the Finance Committee of the Lancashire County Council for 15 years, contributed articles to the accountancy press.

The last of the great canals - the Manchester Ship Canal, constructed 1886-94 - also raised accounting issues. With the problems of the Canal very much in mind, Guthrie argued in favour of allowing the payment of interest out of capital. By the mid 19th century, though, the canals had in general been eclipsed by the railways. Railway accounts and finance provided a number of problems. Dicksee devoted much attention to the so-called double-account system prescribed for railway companies in the 1868 legislation and (e.g.) for gas companies in 1871. The rates charged by the railway companies were a vital element of the costs of 'traders' who had to pay them and they were often contested in courts: Fells was a leading consultant in this area and an expert witness who appeared on the side of the traders.

The First World War

The First World War had a great impact upon the accountancy profession as, of course, it had upon almost all aspects of British life. Many accountants found themselves in the Services or otherwise engaged in government work, Fells and de Paula among them. The importance of cost accounting was more widely recognised and taxation work became for the first time a major part of accounting practice.

The War had another effect on the profession, which has perhaps gone unrecognised. It exaggerated the predominance in accounting education and ideas of the work of Dicksee, Cutforth, de Paula, and, to a lesser extent, Pixley. The issue is simply that the First World War was effective in eliminating, if not a whole generation of young men, at least an important proportion of the generation of young accountants which might have provided replacements in the 1920s and 1930s for men like the pioneers we deal with in this book. Both Pixley and Dicksee lost sons in the War, in Dicksee's case his only child. There were heavy losses of young qualified men and articled clerks as well as of other potential entrants to the profession, and the exhausting War years levied a heavy toll on the minds and energies of serving practitioners. The consequence was that successive editions of pre-War works continued to appear with only limited revision into the 1930s, despite the major changes that were taking place in the economic and social context of business and in the demands falling on the profession.

In conclusion

Accountancy is a practical profession, and over the years accountants have, like other practical men, tended to repeat both the successes and the failures of their founding fathers. We need to remember, amongst other things, that the accountancy profession's very success - its remarkable proven capacity to expand and prosper - has been inclined to isolate many successful specialists within the specialisms they have developed, with the effect that lessons learned by individual leaders or active specialist groups have often (despite the existence of co-ordinating machinery like the professional press and the Students' and District Societies) not been readily communicated to the generality of practitioners. There have been important truths, hardly won, which have been lost and have had to await re-discovery in later periods. Failures of such a kind in the review and transmission of knowledge represent a heavy cost to a fast-growing profession.

The present authors hope and believe that recent developments in the provision of research facilities and in the reporting of research in accounting, along with growth in the study and teaching of accounting in universities and other institutions of higher education in Britain, offer hope of sounder bases for further development, in the future, of accounting education and ideas.

CHAPTER 2

EDWIN GUTHRIE, FCA, 1841-1904

Introduction

'We must', wrote The Accountant on November 8, 1884, 'congratulate the Manchester Society on having for its President a gentleman of Mr. Guthrie's ability. Whilst the Manchester accountants possess such presidents as the one who now rules their destinies there will be no fear of them losing their present position as the foremost provincial Society in the United Kingdom'. The leader writer was perhaps a little too fulsome and he was probably confusing England and Wales with the United Kingdom, but there is no doubt of the impression that Edwin Guthrie made on his contemporaries. He was a man of many parts: a founder member of the Institute of Chartered Accountants in England and Wales and signatory of the royal charter in 1880; President 1884-85 and 1898-99 of the Manchester Society of Chartered Accountants; the catalyst in 1886 for the formation of a body in New York out of which was to grow the American Institute of Certified Public Accountants; President 1888-90 of the Manchester Statistical Society; Chairman of the Finance Committee of the Lancashire County Council from its inception in 1889 to his death in 1904; senior partner of the firm which in 1955 became the Manchester Office of Peat,Marwick,Mitchell & Co. With typical Victorian energy he involved himself in plans for local improvement: writing in 1866 a pamphlet advocating a ferry across the Mersey from Liverpool to Birkenhead; working (without much success) for the merger of Manchester and Salford; supporting (with much more success) the building of the Manchester Ship Canal (of which his firm were the auditors).

Guthrie's career

Although regarded (and rightly so) as very much a 'Manchester man', Edwin Guthrie did not in fact move to Manchester until he was about 30. He was born, apparently in relatively humble circumstances, in Bermondsey, not far from where London Bridge station and the offices of Price Waterhouse and Co now stand, on June 22, 1841. His parents David and Ann Guthrie (nee Barber) then in their early 20s, already had two children (Malcolm and Margaret, born in Marylebone). In 1841 the number was increased to four for Edwin had a twin sister Alice (she later married an accountant). A few years later the family moved to Liverpool, where another son, Herbert, was born on 3 February 1844 in the West Derby district. Nothing is known of Edwin's education. At the time of the 1861 census, when he was 19, the family were still in Liverpool, though not at the same address, and Edwin was working as a bookkeeper to a general merchant. During the late 1860s he appears to have established a business as a contractor in Birkenhead - hence his 1866 pamphlet, which was probably his first published work. Although he does not explicitly say so, the text of the pamphlet suggests that he had already visited New York.

In 1869 he married at St. Michael's Church, Liverpool, Augusta Strong, the daughter of a master mariner of New Brighton. His own occupation is given as estate agent. There were no children of the marriage.

In the early 1870s Guthrie left Liverpool and went into practice in Manchester with John Thomas and Charles Henry Wade. The firm of Thomas, Wade and Guthrie built up a flourishing practice. Neither Wade nor Guthrie, for reasons which are obscure, joined the Manchester Institute of Accountants formed on February 6, 1871. In 1878, however, Wade and Guthrie formed the Accountants' Incorporation Association to protect the interests of those not members of any existing accounting body. The draft petition for a Royal Charter was signed by the Presidents of the Institute of Accountants, the Society of Accountants in England, the Manchester and Sheffield Institutes, and the Liverpool Society, and by Guthrie and Wade on behalf of the Association. Guthrie became a Fellow of the newly-formed Institute of Chartered Accountants in England and Wales on 11 May, 1880. He remained throughout his life a member of its Council.

Guthrie was also involved with the establishment of the American Association of Public Accountants, the first such association in the United States and one of the predecessor bodies of the American Institute of Certified Public Accountants.

It is not known when he first visited New York but he was there as a receiver in 1883 when the firm of Barrow, Wade, Guthrie & Co, was founded. It was the first British accounting firm in New York. The resident partner in the USA was John Wylie Barrow, a cousin of Charles Dickens. Barrow died in 1885 (there is an obituary in The Accountant, 30 May 1885) and whilst Guthrie was visiting New York in December 1886 he proposed at a meeting of public accountants held in the firm's offices that American accountants should organise themselves as British accountants had already done but that they should not describe themselves as chartered accountants. The idea was received enthusiastically and the American Association of Public Accountants was formed. (The Accountant, 15 January 1887, p.31 and James T. Anyon, Recollections of the Early Days of American Accountancy 1883-1893, 1925, repr. 1974, pp.9-19.)

A London office was opened by Guthrie's firm in 1886 and Chicago and San Francisco offices in 1894 and 1895. In 1895 Wade and Guthrie separated (The Accountant, 5 October 1895, p.791) and Guthrie's firm was known as Edwin Guthrie & Co until its absorption by Peat, Marwick, Mitchell in 1955.

From 1876 to 1904 Guthrie lived in the prestigious suburb of Victoria Park of whose Trust Committee he became chairman. Victoria Park, a private estate with toll-gates and keepers in uniform, is described by A.J.P. Taylor in an article in Encounter (March 1957) as the most revealing spot in Manchester:

> Gothic palaces jostle each other; gardeners dust the soot from the leaves of the trees; and the ghosts of merchant princes walk in the twilight. These were the men who gave Manchester its historical character. We think of them in retrospect as Radicals; and so they were in lack of respect for traditional authority or in their ruthless destruction of whatever stood in their way. But they were far from a belief in economic equality or even in democracy, if we mean by that putting the needs of the majority first. They had succeeded by their own energy; and they supposed that the duty of society was discharged if it gave others the chance to do the same. It did not worry them that, while the rich man was in his mansion, the poor man at the gates of Victoria Park lived in a slum. The road to success lay open for those who wished to take it. Like the men of the Renaissance they exalted the individual.

Taylor's vivid description fits Guthrie well, although it must be mentioned in fairness that Guthrie was a director of and shareholder in the Manchester Labourers' Dwelling Co. Ltd.

It is said that as a professional man in Manchester Guthrie specialised in being in the right places at the right time: in the Constitutional Club and at the Halle Concert on Thursday evening.

Guthrie was intimately involved in the Liberal politics of late 19th century Manchester and Lancashire. He was chairman of the Finance Committee of the Lancashire County Council from its formation in 1889 to his death in 1904. His budget speeches became locally famous. The Accountant's obituary (3 September 1904) refers to him as 'practically Lancashire's Chancellor of the Exchequer' and adds that he possessed the rare power to make figures interesting to his hearers.

Guthrie was an enthusiastic member of the Manchester Statistical Society, serving as a member of its council from 1880 until his death in 1904 and as president 1888-1890. His inaugural address as president, which was reprinted in The Accountant of February 9 1889 is an interesting statement of his economic, social and political views. He also delivered papers to the Society on the decimal system as applied to coinage, weights and measures; the effects upon trade of 'cornering' in relation to commodities; state socialism and individualism; local government; and local taxation (the last was reprinted in The Accountant of March 16, 1895).

This is not the place to pursue Guthrie in all his interests, although it is to be hoped that one day he will find a biographer. The emphasis in this chapter must be on his contribution to accounting thought and more especially on the series of articles he wrote in which we can see the origins of much of present day accounting thought and practice. We shall pay particular attention to his views on uniformity, depreciation, local authority accounts and the payment of interest out of capital. We shall also look briefly at his views on a number of other accounting matters.

Uniformity

Guthrie's first published article on accounting was on 'The want of uniformity in accounts' or, to give it its full title, 'The want of uniformity in the modes of stating accounts; the frequency of inconsistency between the title and subject-matter of published accounts, and the employment of non-correlative terms in accounts'. It was read at a meeting of the Manchester Society of Chartered Accountants on 20 October 1882 and printed in The Accountant of 28 October and aroused considerable interest.

Guthrie was concerned with the lack of uniformity in naming and presenting the two principal financial statements. He saw this not as a matter of principle but of usage and convenience and argued that once an arbitrary election had been made 'it will surely be most convenient and consistent that it be adhered to in all its reproductions'. He therefore argued that published Profit and Loss Accounts should follow the form of the ledger account. He also asked: 'On which side should the Assets appear on a Balance Sheet, and consequently on which side the Liabilities? Many English Accountants to whom I have put the question have answered without hesitation - the Liabilities on the Left and the Assets on the Right, and with this dismiss the question as beyond controversy'. Guthrie notes, however, that the reverse form is almost universal in other countries and that uniformity is not complete in England. Again he argues that the balance sheet is a condensation of the ledger: 'Why in the process of condensation, the balance should change sides is for someone else to explain. I cannot'.*

Continuing, Guthrie condemns the practice of confusing and mixing the titles of Receipts and Payments Accounts and Income and Expenditure Accounts. He also advocates distinguishing in Profit and Loss Accounts between the principal activities and supplementary activities. Finally he recommends that stock in the profit and loss account should be 'merged in the respective accounts of cost', i.e. shown as part of cost of goods sold or cost manufactured: 'In trades dealing with a single commodity, as, for instance Coal or Cotton, this form permits the working out on the face of the account of the cost per ton or per pound in respect of each element of cost.'

Guthrie's papers were always well researched and well illustrated. Ten examples of accounts - some real, some made up - are appended to his published paper. At the Manchester meeting he also laid upon the table 'a number of accounts and Balances of Foreign countries, - French, German, Italian, Russian, Scandinavian, American and others.'

Table 1 reproduces his other appendix: the list of works on bookkeeping he consulted on the mode of placing assets and liabilities in balance sheets. A rather similar list was later used by the Scottish writer Lisle in his article on balance sheets in The Accountants Encyclopaedia, (to which Guthrie contributed the section on depreciation). Whether Guthrie possessed copies of all these books himself there is unfortunately no means of knowing.

The discussion and letters which followed Guthrie's paper concentrated largely on which side of the balance sheet the assets and liabilities should respectively be placed, and it was even suggested that a resolution should be passed on the subject. David Chadwick, FCA, MP, a leading Manchester practitioner, stated, however: 'This is a very old question with me, because I have been discussing it for about thirty years; and I confess that I do not place anything like the same amount of importance to the placing of liabilities and assets on the one side or the other, neither do I think it would be worthy of ourselves to pass a resolution on the subject ... make your balance sheet correct, and it does not matter on which side you place your assets or liabilities'. He expressed himself disappointed that Guthrie had not given an account of the views of previous writers and described some of his references

---

* This question is discussed by B.S. Yamey in his article 'Closing the Ledger', Accounting and Business Research, vol.1, 1970, pp.71-77.

TABLE 1

Mode of placing Assets and Liabilities in Balance Sheets, as adopted by some of English Authors of Works on Book-keeping.

AUTHOR.	Date.	TITLE.	MODE OF PLACING.
William Webster	1721	Essay on Book-keeping	"Ballence" Dr. Debts due) (Debts owing to me.) (Cr. by me.
Chas. Hutton, LL.D., F.R.S.	1810	A complete Treatise on Book-keeping	Balance. Assets - Liabilities.
Ree's Cyclopaedia	1819	Article on Book-keeping	Balance. Assets - Liabilities.
James Morrison	1825	The Elements of Book-keeping	Balance. Assets - Liabilities.
C. Morrison	1834	A complete system of Practical Book-keeping	Balance Account. Assets - Liabilities.
Isaac Preston Cory	1839	Practical Treatise on Accounts	Balance Account. Assets - Liabilities.
J. Caldecott	1850	Practical Guide to Account-keeping	Balance Account. Assets - Liabilities.
B. F. Foster	1852	Double Entry elucidated	Balance Sheet. Assets - Liabilities.
W. Inglis	1858	Book-keeping	Balance Sheet. Liabilities - Assets.
With a remark that "In some systems the Balance Sheet is Dr. Assets Cr. Liabilities, the positions being reversed."			
James Haddon	1859	Rudimentary Book-keeping	Balance Account. Assets - Liabilities.
R. S. E. Farries	1865	Joint Stock Companies	Balance Sheet. Liabilities - Assets.
Rev. J. Hunter	1868	Book-keeping	Balance Sheet. Assets - Liabilities.
D. Macdougal	-	A complete system of Book-keeping	Balance Sheet. Liabilities - Assets.
			Specimen of Balance Sheet, as drawn up for a Limited Liability Co. Liabilities - Assets.
F. Hayne Carter	-	Book-keeping	Specimen of Balance Sheet, as drawn up for a Private Trading Co. Assets - Liabilities.
R. Y. Barnes	1871	Universal system of Book-keeping	Balance Sheet. Liabilities - Assets.
Hy. Manly	1875	Book-keeping	Balance Sheet. Assets - Liabilities.
Hamilton and Ball	1876	Book-keeping	Balance Sheet. Liabilities - Assets.
James Haddon	1879	Book-keeping	Balance Sheet. Liabilities - Assets.
J. H. Webber	1880	Book-keeper's Companion	Balance Sheet. Liabilities - Assets.
Arthur Eldridge, F.C.A.	1882	Kain's Commercial Book-keeping	Balance Sheet. Assets - Liabilities.

as 'merely shilling books on accounts'. This was rather unfair. Previous writers do not appear to have discussed the question and textbooks on accounting as distinct from bookkeeping had scarcely yet been published: Pixley's Auditors, which can be considered the first of these, had only appeared the year before, in 1881.

Chadwick went on to praise the accounts prescribed in the Regulation of Railways Act of 1868: 'There you have absolute conformity compulsorily made'. Nobody in the discussion seriously disputed the desirability of uniformity, though they differed as to what uniform accounts should look like,and the debate ended with the unanimous resolution: 'That it is desirable that the accounts of joint-stock companies and public bodies be stated in a uniform manner, which should be compulsory'.

The debate was continued in a series of letters to The Accountant during 1882 and 1883. The most distinguished correspondent was George Walter Knox of Sheffield. 'All will be agreed', he wrote in the issue of November 25, 1882, 'as to the desirability of uniformity in the presentation of statements of account so far as the form of the account is concerned'. He brought out more clearly the implicit entity/proprietary distinction in the argument: 'a distinction has to be made between A.B. the firm, viz. in his capacity of carrying on the particular business, and A.B. the individual who has capital in it'.

The most striking feature of the debate compared with those on the subject more recently is the lack of any doubt that although published accounts were not uniform they ought to be. Much later Guthrie stated, to the applause of his audience of chartered accountants, that it was government requirements which had caused such a diversity of the methods in which the accounts of municipal corporations had been kept, and that this was one of the striking indications of the unfitness or incapacity of the government to deal with matters affecting the accountant's profession (see The Accountant, 17 October, 1896, p.862 and November 14, 1896, p.931).

Depreciation

Guthrie's paper on 'Depreciation and Sinking Funds' was read to a meeting of the Manchester Accountants' Students' Society on April 2, 1883, and published in The Accountant of April 21. It is the first fully reported paper on the subject. It has been reprinted in Richard P. Brief (ed.), The Late

Nineteenth Century Debate over Depreciation, Capital and Income (New York: Arno Press, 1976).

Guthrie begins by pointing out that machinery and buildings are consumed by a manufacturing business just as materials and labour are but the difference is that they are consumed over a number of years. Neither the precise value consumed nor the residue of value carried forward from year to year is exactly measurable. The life of the machine or building has therefore to be estimated.

For leased land and buildings he recommends the straight line method (although he does not call it that) on the grounds that the larger burden of interest incurred in the earlier years is generally counterbalanced by the additional cost of repairs in the later years.

For moveable machinery he recommends the reducing balance method (although again he does not use the phrase) mainly on the grounds that the ratio of diminution of realisable value is greater in the earlier than in the later years of life of machinery. He rejects, however, on 'going concern' grounds, realisable value as a principle of valuation at the end of each accounting period. Only the realisable value at the end of a whole term is relevant since 'manufacturers and traders do not construct business premises or lay down special plant in the intent of a short period.'

He is not, however, advocating historical cost since in his next paragraph he envisages periodic revaluations, but 'made with regard to normal cost rather than to the value on the day of valuation' for 'matter and things fixed in a permanent working position must not be treated in accounts as following the fluctuations of the market.'

In any case of uncertainty higher rather than lower rates of depreciation are safer but too great a charge should be avoided because it may lead to selling prices being fixed too high. It may be fairest and most prudent to capitalise and depreciate irregular repair charges. The article includes a useful table of depreciation rates for different types of assets.

Guthrie's conclusion is that the 'actuarial principle, applied upon bases arbitrarily settled by the exercise of judgment founded on experience, settles the great guiding rule in the rating of depreciation.'

Towards the end of his life Guthrie contributed an article on depreciation to Lisle's Encyclopaedia of Accounting. Whilst dealing with many practical matters, it adds little to principle. Depreciation is defined as 'the measure as between an earlier and later date, of the reduction in value of any given property' and 'an element in the cost of manufacture represented by the deterioration by wear and tear, decay, or reduction in value arising by reason of age and use of buildings, fixed and loose machinery and plant of every description employed in the production of things produced for sale or disposal in the ordinary way of trade.' He again considers periodical valuations desirable to verify the sufficiency of rates of depreciation and again favours the reducing balance method:

> the most preferable method of treating depreciation is the charging of a given rate over the whole period of the life of the plant, charged, not on the original value, but on the diminishing value. This method recognises the fact that there is always a residue of value, and also the fact that machinery diminishes, in realisable value, in a greater amount as between the time of its first installation and the end of the first year's working than in any other year. So that this method has the merit both of recognising the residue of value, and, in the incidence of the charge, follows the actual as well as the theoretical ratio of reduced value.

He is at pains to point out that local authority accounts ought not to confuse depreciation with loan repayments:

> The loan out of which the works have been erected has been borrowed from some person or persons who have simply got to be paid off. The money wherewith the creditors have to be repaid has to be found by the ratepayers, either out of the profit of the undertaking or by a specific rate. In any case the property is the property of the local authority at its value, and its value is the amount expended upon it, less its depreciation, and the balance is the amount of the permanent asset representing permanent capital, and, accurately treated, should appear in the balance-sheet, although the loan and the interest thereupon has been wholly repaid and the personal accounts extinguished.

Local authority accounts

Local authority accounts were of great interest to Guthrie. He was, as already noted, chairman of the finance committee of Lancashire County Council from 1889 to 1904. His firm were for a time auditors of the Manchester Corporation. His most substantial contribution to the literature on the subject was a paper read in his absence (he was in New York at the time) by his partner C. H. Wade to the first autumnal meeting of the English Institute in 1886, held in Manchester. The paper was published in The Accountant of 30 October, 1886.

The paper is divided into three parts: historical (<u>The Accountant</u> in a leader of December 11, 1886 regretted that 'so much valuable space should be taken up with what purports to be an historical review'); statistical (very brief); and technical. In the technical section he argued for making a clear distinction in the accounts between the non-trading and the trading departments; that balance sheets and income and expenditure accounts were preferable to mere receipts and payments accounts; and against the want of uniformity as between the inclusion and exclusion of assets of certain kinds in municipal corporation balance sheets.

He argued that the only basis of valuation of an <u>unrealisable property</u> (e.g. Manchester Town Hall which had been built 1868-1877 and in which the meeting took place) was cost. Guthrie's arguments here are worth reproducing in some detail:

> I differ from the recent action of the Corporation, who have, by a standing order, directed that henceforth a quinquennial valuation of all the property of the Corporation shall be made. That order was carried out for the first time this year, and the amounts of the valuation introduced into the last published accounts for the first time with the effect of introducing a very disturbing and dangerous element.
>
> The element is a disturbing one, for the account formerly showed on the one hand (a) the actual cost of the property and on the other (b) the amount of the balance of the indebtedness incurred in respect of the expenditure, (c) the amount of the extent by which the original sum borrowed had been reduced; but by the new order the points of the true history of the financing of the Town Hall is destroyed by the introduction of a fiction.
>
> In the case of the palace in which we are now met, of what avail is it, I ask, to say that its value is any particular sum. Is it a realisable value? I do not think anyone will claim that it is. Of what utility is it to say that it is worth only £730,000, and not £800,000? It is not surely supposed that we could sell it for either one sum or the other. I apprehend that the condition of things under which the Manchester Town Hall might be submitted for conversion into cash would be the condition of the accomplished ruin of the trade and city of Manchester, when it would be worth nothing, but along with all other property in the city would be abandoned to decay.
> On the other hand there is a good reason why the Town Hall should have been allowed to stand at the £800,000. That balance was based upon actual cost. What other test of the value is there of an unrealisable property? At the time that a property is acquired it is supposed to be worth what it will cost, otherwise it would not be acquired. I repeat, there is no other test of value of non-revenue bearing and unrealisable public property. Any other valuation is fictitious.
>
> ....
>
> If the practice of quinquennial valuations should be adhered to, the accounts will be subject to unusual and unnatural effects, and from

time to time to fluctuations of figures, based upon two intangible elements; first the state of the property market for the time being - a market to which property in the permanent occupation of the Corporation is not subject - and secondly, to the personal opinion of the valuer for the time being, and that, in respect of property, having to a great extent no practicable realisable value, in respect of which the best opinion is of doubtful service.

....

These remarks do not, of course, apply to the trading departments or to revenue-bearing properties, which have a market value, and may be disposed of without hindrance to the efficient performance of the functions of the Corporation as such.

....

In my opinion it would be distinctly preferable that all property in the permanent occupation or use of Corporations should stand only in the accounts so long as they represent a set-off to certain specific indebtedness in respect of them, and that they should then appear only upon a supplementary schedule of unrealised property.

Finally he argued that the audits of municipal corporations should preferably be conducted by chartered accountants, rather than by elective auditors or government officials (Guthrie was actively involved with the County Councils' Association which was trying to achieve a similar result (see for example, the report in The Accountant of 9 April, 1892).

Guthrie's views on municipal balance sheets were succinctly set out by him in a letter to The Accountant of April 6, 1895:

That every municipality and other public authority ought to produce a Balance Sheet.

That such Balance Sheet ought to distinguish between revenue-bearing and non-revenue-bearing property, and as to whether the respective properties be of a realisable or non-realisable nature.

That the true value, so far as ascertainable, should be given.

That, generally, the true test of value is the cost of acquisition, so far as any value remains.

> This rule of the cost being the test of value would be departed from, for instance, in such a case as the acquisition of a plot of land, the greater portion of which was converted into street or open space. In that case the residue of the land available for realisation should be valued.

That property subject to wear and tear - and this applies especially to trading concerns, such as gasworks - should be subject to depreciation rated according to the expectation of 'life'.

That the redemption of loans and depreciation are two separate and distinct elements, and have no necessary relations to each other, loans being personal accounts redeemable generally out of revenue, such revenue becoming capitalised to the extent of the residual value, as appearing in the capital, or surplus, or common fund, or whatever the balance to the good as between assets and liabilities may be called; whilst depreciation is an impersonal charge going in reduction of particular assets, and in corresponding reduction of the capital, surplus, or common fund.

That in such cases as where a loan is taken for the purpose of construction of some non-revenue-bearing and unrealisable works of a sunk or wasting value, the asset should appear in the Balance Sheet at its annually diminishing sum corresponding with the balance of liability upon loan, and eventually disappear in the same way as, say, the formation expenses of a company. I should then give place to assets so disappearing by way of schedule or memorandum appended to the Balance Sheet; but I certainly should not advocate such assets as paving and sewering appearing in the Balance Sheet itself before striking the balance and finding the surplus.

Guthrie also read a paper on municipal accounts and their audit to the Bristol Society of Chartered Accountants. This was printed in the Incorporated Accountants' Journal of February 1904 (pp.111-116). He again argued for accrual rather than cash accounting and for improved terminology. He stressed the difference between depreciation and a sinking fund charge:

> Depreciation is an element appertaining to trading or profit and loss account. The sinking fund charge is an element of capital redeemed out of profits or rates, as the case may be ... depreciation and sinking funds are not tied together in any way (pp.113-4).

Finally he called again for professional audits by chartered accountants (the Journal in a leader was concerned to include incorporated accountants as well).

Payment of interest out of capital

Guthrie's lecture on the payment of interest on capital during construction of works was read to the Manchester Society of Chartered Accountants at a meeting of the Society held on January 29, 1886. It was printed as a pamphlet and also published in The Accountant of February 13 and 20 of the same year. The date is important. The Manchester Ship Canal Company, of which Thomas, Wade, Guthrie and Co. were auditors, had been incorporated by a private Act of Parliament the previous year. The canal was built between 1886 and 1894 at a cost of £14 million and its early days were financially precarious. Guthrie's lecture must be considered in this context.

He gave three reasons for considering the subject: (i) as a matter of principle (ii) as a matter of policy and (iii) as a matter of local interest. He devotes the first part of his paper to the legislation affecting the question.

The Companies Clauses Consolidation Act, 1845 prohibited payment of dividends or interest out of capital and as a consequence of the railway crisis the House of Commons and the House of Lords adopted in 1847 Standing Orders barring the introduction of any Bill into Parliament without a prohibitory clause. The Standing Order of the House of Commons was, however, modified in 1883 to allow such clauses in particular cases. The Companies Act of 1862 contained no such prohibition. (The present law, as embodied in s.65 of the Companies Act, 1948 dates from 1907.)

Guthrie then turned to the accounting and financial principles involved and argued that it was anomalous to accept interest as an element of cost where a property was acquired by purchase and not to accept it where the property was constructed by the company itself: 'I contend that interest is as much earned upon the proprietors' as upon the borrowed capital, and although the objection, that a man cannot earn money from himself, and pay himself with his own money, appears plausible, it is but superficially plausible and nothing more'. Interest was he argued paid <u>not</u> out of capital but <u>upon</u> capital.

Moving to policy considerations he claimed that the legal constraints had not been effective but 'subterfuge and evasion, the inevitable consequents of all unhealthy restraints /a typical expression of Guthrie's general philosophy!/, have been brought into play, and that at great cost to the community, who have always to bear the penalty resulting from the application of laws in contravention of free economy'. The restraints were evaded by the bulk of new railway undertakings being carried out by old companies who could, through the medium of their already large accounts of capital, borrowing powers, revenues, by arrangements with their contractors, and since the Railway Regulations Act 1868 by the issue of new capital at a discount, so cover up the element of cost represented by interest that, whether visible or invisible it was there, and dividends could be paid upon new capital.

New companies also learned how to evade the restraints, e.g. by providing that the contractors should provide the necessary sum for the payment of interest; by means of the receipt of money in advance of calls; or by the issue of shares at a discount.

He concluded with a plea that the Manchester Ship Canal Company should not be prohibited from paying interest on capital during construction.

In the discussion that followed it was argued, not without justification, that the paper was 'prepared with that species of ingenuity which was always required to establish an impossible proposition'. Guthrie was clearly pleading a special case.

Other accounting matters

Guthrie also wrote at some length on goodwill (The Accountant, April 23, 1898) but he contributed nothing original. In a paper on 'Some Controversial Points in Accounts' (The Accountant, October 22, 1898) he touched on wasting assets (condemning the decision in Lee v. The Neuchatel Asphalte Company), goodwill, the accounts of insurance companies, revaluation of securities, interest on capital, hidden reserves and reserve funds. Claiming that the undervaluation of assets is much less frequent than their overvaluation, he concluded that 'common-sense would assume that, so long as any such undervaluation is only prudential, and not so excessive as to substantially affect in an adverse sense the selling value of an individual proprietor's interests, such extra reserves as those in question may be not only held to be free from condemnation, but even to be commended' (p.994).

Guthrie wrote little on cost accounting matters but the following quotation, taken from his 1878 pamphlet Bad Trade Considered in Relation to the Present Condition of the Cotton Industry in England and repeated in his 1883 pamphlet The Cotton Trade: Its Conditions and Prospects, shows his awareness of the distinction between controllable ('elastic') and uncontrollable ('rigid') costs:

> It will be perceived that of all the elements of cost certain of these elements are more or less rigid, and in treating the matter as one of competition between localities, it is important to recognise the various qualities of rigidity and elasticity of these elements. The first named, viz, cost of cotton, is of the first degree of rigidity between the various buyers, for they are customers of the same market, and the cost of carriage to the mills is becoming rapidly equalised. The second element of cost, viz, mills and machinery, is, so far as present erections go, absolutely rigid and unalterable as an annual charge over the whole production, or non-production, of each mill. But in respect of the number of hours worked and consequent production, it is elastic and variable, favourably as the hours of labour and quantity of production are increased, and vice versa. The third element, namely, cost of power, may be regarded as rigid; at all events it is not within the direct control of the spinner. The fourth element, viz, the cost of labour, is again an elastic one, and may be made to vary at the will of the workers. The fifth element, viz, the cost of reaching the customers, may also be treated as a rigid one, not being within the control of the spinner.
>
> Of the five elements of cost we have thus three of them rigid and not within the control of the manufacturer in any appreciable degree, and we have two elastic elements, viz, first, cost of mill and machinery, commuted under the terms rent, interest, and depreciation; secondly, the price of labour. In the question of the competition

> between different localities in which the trade can be carried on, these - except in a very small degree - are the only voluntarily variable elements of cost, and if those who have these elements of cost under their control will not submit to variation under pressure, profits must disappear, sales reduce, stocks accumulate, and bad trade - that is, the impeded circulation and interchange of commodities - must settle upon the community.

Guthrie was a prominent member of the Decimal Association and strongly favoured decimalisation of the currency and a change over to the metric system. The Accountant in 1891 regarded such an alternative as 'inevitable' at 'no distant date'. In the ICAEW's centenary year the former has been achieved but the latter has still some way to go. He read a paper on the decimal system to the Manchester Statistical Society in 1880. In 1884 (his presidential year) he lectured to the Manchester Society of Chartered Accountants on the development of the art of numeration, his talk being accompanied by an exhibition of instruments, tables and other mechanical aids to calculation. These included a small original portion of Babbage's 'difference engine'. The talk concluded with a plea for the adoption of the decimal and metric systems and the abandonment of 'a complicated and irrational system of pricing, weighing and measuring'.

Guthrie's contribution

Guthrie died in 1904 in Broughton Old Hall, Salford, to which he had recently moved from Victoria Park. His contribution to the accounting profession was very much that of a pioneer. He was unique in taking part in the foundation of both the English and American Institutes. He built up an important professional practice. He was not a writer of text books but his published papers show an originality and an emphasis on principle often lacking in his contemporaries and successors. He was very much of his age but the twentieth century profession owes much to his efforts.

CHAPTER 3

FRANCIS WILLIAM PIXLEY, VD, FSA, JP, FCA
1852-1933

Francis William Pixley is best known today as the author of the first British text on auditing. Auditors: Their Duties and Responsibilities was first published in 1881 and went through twelve editions, the last being in 1922. It was reprinted by the Arno Press, New York in 1976. He was also the author of numerous other books on accounting and related subjects, notably The Shareholders' Handbook (1884), The Duties and Powers of Trustees, Official Receivers, Managers, and Committees of Inspection, under the Bankruptcy Act, 1883 (1884), Chartered Accountants' Charges and the Law Relating Thereto (1st edition 1889), The Profession of a Chartered Accountant (revised versions of papers written 1883-1896, published 1897 and reprinted by the Arno Press in 1978), How to Read the Balance Sheet of a Commercial Concern (1st edition 1906), Accountancy (1st edition 1908) and Clubs and their Management (1st edition 1916). He was the co-author of a work on Book-keeping (1892) and editor of The Accountant's Dictionary (1st edition 1922). Pixley's influence through his writings was not so great as Dicksee's but he was more prominent as a practitioner, becoming president of the Institute of Chartered Accountants in England and Wales in 1903-1904. When he died in 1933, aged 80, he was the Institute's senior past president.

What accountants do today is still, whether they know it or not, conditioned by the reactions of the pioneers such as Pixley to the circumstances in which they found themselves and by the type of men they were. In his perceptive preface to The English View of Accountants' Duties and Responsibilities 1881-1902 (Arno Press, 1978) the editor, Michael Chatfield, expresses the view that 'men such as Dicksee, Pixley, Cooper and Lowes Dickinson have influenced modern accounting thought more than almost anyone alive today. They came on the scene just at the time when accounting practice required codification, and they seized a unique opportunity to set standards for future generations of accountants.'

That Pixley was aware of and welcomed such an opportunity is clear from the paper he gave at the First International Congress of Accountants held at the World's Fair, Saint Louis, in September 1904. The paper is published in the Official Record of the Proceedings of the Congress of Accountants (reprinted in 1978 by the Arno Press). Pixley at this date was the immediate past president of the Institute of Chartered Accountants in England and Wales and was welcomed at the Congress as one who through his writings was known very extensively among American accountants and who had done in that respect a very great service to accountants all over the world. Two of the opening paragraphs of Pixley's paper are worth quoting in full:

> Proud as are the members of some professions of their antiquity, of customs carefully preserved although in many instances out of date, yet to assist in the establishment of a new profession, to feel you are one of those helping to form the professional character of those to follow in your footsteps, to be, in fact, one of the fathers of a profession, appeals to me, as I am sure it does to you, more than to merely step into the shoes of those who have gone before, and to follow a beaten path out of which it is unwise to stray.
> We - and I am speaking for our professional brethren on the other side of the Atlantic as well as for the members of those Societies forming the Federation under whose auspices is assembled this great Congress - are making this beaten path for others to follow. I am sure you will agree with me that a heavy responsibility consequently rests upon us, as the doctrines we lay down for ourselves to follow must necessarily not only have a great and abiding influence on our successors, but also show the financial and commercial community of the present day whether they can confidently entrust us with the great and important duties we profess to transact, so as to secure for ourselves and our successors that general feeling of confidence without which no profession can flourish even for a time, much less endure, as we hope ours will, in the ages to come. (_Congress of Accountants_, pp.122-3).

The profession to which Pixley belonged was, of course, new and much less well known than it is now. It was also small. At the 1904 Congress, Pixley reported that there were 3,200 English chartered accountants, 850 Scottish chartered accountants and 70 Irish chartered accountants (_Congress of Accountants_, p.124). He did not report on the number of incorporated accountants. James Martin, the secretary of the Incorporated Society, who was also at the Congress, stated it to be 2,086 (p.166).

Family background and early career

Pixley was indeed, in his own words, one of the fathers of the new profession. He was born in Victoria Road, South Kensington, on 5 July 1852. The Pixley family was descended from a William Pixley born in Ipswich, Suffolk, c. 1679. William's great-grandson, another William (1787-1869), and grandfather of Francis William, was an elder brother of Trinity House and a ship's captain in the West India trade. His adventurous career is narrated by Captain W.R. Chaplin in _The American Neptune_ of April 1954. He married Charlotte Ellis of

Mr. F. W. PIXLEY, F.C.A.

From *The Accountant*, 17 June 1922

Ipswich in 1812. Late in life he moved to Kensington. His son Thomas William (born 1819) was a master mariner, became a younger brother of Trinity House and married at All Saints, Poplar, in 1848, Caroline Blore, the daughter of a wine merchant. Francis William, their only son, was born four years later. At this date his father was master of the Devonshire engaged in the East India trade. Francis was educated at St. Peter's School, York, Keir House, Wimbledon, and by the Rev. Dr. Frost of Kensington Square, a well-known army tutor. He was intended for the army but failed to pass the eyesight test. This decision was later reversed on appeal but meanwhile he had accepted an appointment in Madras and he stayed there 1871-73 holding a commission in the Volunteer Guards. On returning to England he was introduced to George Chandler (born 1827). In 1878 at the age of 26 Pixley became an Associate of the Institute of Accountants (it is unlikely that he sat any examinations) and joined Chandler in partnership at 24 Moorgate Street.

The Institute of Accountants was the most important of the predecessor bodies of the Institute of Chartered Accountants in England and Wales (ICAEW) formed in 1880. Pixley became a founder member of the new Chartered Institute and was quickly elected a fellow. In the same year he married Elizabeth Mary Simpson, the daughter of a London and Ceylon merchant, at Trinity Church, Kensington. Of their five sons and three daughters, one son was killed in action during the First World War, another died at Cork Barracks in 1903 after having served in the Boer War, and a third died in infancy. In 1889 Chandler died and two years later Pixley merged his practice with another firm to form Jackson, Pixley, Browning, Husey and Co. (later to be known as Jackson, Pixley & Co. and one of the predecessors of the today's leading firm of Clark Pixley).

From Pixley's prolific writings on accounting it is possible to pick out five recurring themes:

(a) a pride in the profession of a chartered accountant;
(b) a belief in the central role of auditing in an accountant's work;
(c) an emphasis on the legal framework;
(d) a practical, non-theoretical approach to accounting;
(e) an emphasis on prudence and the going concern.

Chartered accountancy

Pixley was quite clear as to the need for the new profession. He explained to the Chartered Accountants' Students' Society of London in 1885 (The Profession

<u>of a Chartered Accountant</u>, Lecture 1) how before the grant of the Charter in England many practising accountants were 'destitute alike of moral principles as of business capabilities'. In a later paper to the same body (Lecture 5, originally delivered in 1894) he admitted that the ICAEW included some incapable auditors in its ranks because it was felt to be unfair to exclude anyone who at the date of the Charter was in practice. However:

> Those who have been articled to our members since the date of the Charter come from the same class as do those who are now at Woolwich, Sandhurst, and the Inns of Court. They have been educated at the same class of schools, and, in addition, they have had a special education in the duties of Auditors. (p.128)

Since those entering articles had to pay not only a premium but also the solicitor's cost of the preparation of the articles (Lecture 1,p.5) this (to modern readers) rather unattractive statement may well be true. Pixley's own sons were educated at Eton.

Pixley regretted that the Charter did not contain clauses preventing anyone from practising in Great Britain who did not within a reasonable time become a member of the English Institute or of one of the Scottish societies (<u>Accountancy</u>, p.33).

It was the view of <u>The Pall Mall Gazette</u> in 1890 that it was 'unadvisable and altogether imprudent' to become a chartered accountant unless one had a capital of at least £2,000 or £3,000 (say £40,000 or £60,000 in 1980 terms) or influential friends in business circles: 'The two combined is desirable, but the latter the more important' (see <u>The Accountant</u>, 20 September 1890, pp.499-500). In the same year the <u>Bankers Magazine</u> carried a biographical note of Pixley's career to date and stated that as 'A member of the Conservative and City of London Clubs, he is closely connected, by family and association, with what is most solid and of best standing in the mercantile world'. His family connections included an uncle, Robert Ellis Pixley, who was a stockbroker at 8 Copthall Court, Throgmorton Street and another uncle, Stewart Pixley, who was a bullion broker. In 1917 he was to become Auditor to the Duchy of Lancaster, a post which has continued to be held by a partner in his firm.

Pixley did not feel that the duties devolving on a chartered accountant were suitable for all intellects: 'They are most likely to succeed in the profession who at school or college select mathematics for their principal study in preference to classics. It is not only extremely possible, but most probable, that the men /there were, of course, no potential women chartered accountants at this date/ who take high honours in the latter would be very unlikely to take an interest in the work of a professional Accountant.' (Lecture 1, p.3). Today, perhaps, Pixley would be a strong supporter of relevant degrees!

Not unnaturally he disapproved strongly of non-professional auditors. In a paper delivered in 1887 he noted with satisfaction that the 'revelations which have been made in the Courts' had so startled the financial world that the amateur auditor was fast dying out (Lecture IV, p.67). (The reference is to the case of Leeds Estate Building and Investment Co. v. Shepherd where the auditor, who was a bank clerk, was found to be negligent when failing to ensure that the audited balance sheet was drawn up in accordance with the company's articles of association). He points out on several occasions the need to legislate for compulsory audit for all companies. This was not to come until 1900 although the Companies Act of 1879 had, following the failure of the City of Glasgow Bank in 1878, introduced such a requirement for banking companies. The commercial depression of 1866 had, however, persuaded the business community to turn towards the professional accountant (Congress of Accountants, p.134). (1866 was the year of the Overend Gurney crash.)

Legislation should, he argued, state a little more clearly the duties of auditors and should make auditors independent. Given this, auditors will carry out those duties: 'I say more, it is we alone who can carry them out'. (Lecture V, p.128).

He regarded professional accountants as well able to compete with other professionals. It was, he claimed, recognised that they were 'desirable candidates for appointments of every description where business-like attainments, knowledge of office management, and accountancy are considered essential qualifications' (Accountancy, p.44).

Auditing

Although many textbooks on bookkeeping were available, there were, when the English Institute received its charter in 1880, none on auditing and it is Pixley's enduring claim to fame that he wrote the first text on the subject in 1881 at the early age of 29.

When the Charter was granted in 1880 auditing was not regarded as the most important branch of a professional accountant's work. The words of the Charter itself placed greater emphasis on liquidations, receiverships and trusteeships. To Pixley, however, auditing was the mainstay of a chartered accountant's practice. Investigation of accounts, most of the work connected with liquidations and trusteeships in bankruptcy, reporting upon the accounts of executors, giving evidence as an expert witness: all required a knowledge of auditing (Lecture IV, pp.66-67).

Some of Pixley's views on auditing sound rather primitive today: the purpose of an audit is to enable the auditor to 'certify as to the accuracy of the Accounts presented' (Auditors, 1st ed. p.92, repeated in later editions); an auditor's signature after the single word 'audited' is the strongest he can give and 'implies that without a single reservation the accounts are correct in every particular' (Lecture IV, p.87).

Some appear to strike a more modern note. He was convinced that it was a mistake for an auditor to be a shareholder: partly because shareholder auditors were likely to be incompetent amateurs but partly also because they might fail in duties through selfish motives (Auditors, 1st ed., pp.152-3). There was also no doubt an element of self-interest in such a view.

Accounting and the law

Throughout Pixley's writings there is an emphasis on the law. In this he was well versed, being called to the Bar in 1894 (not 1904 as incorrectly stated in his obituary in The Accountant, 6 May 1933). He regarded the clientele of a chartered accountant as being practically the same as that of a barrister (Lecture 1, p.3). Large portions of Auditors: Their Duties and Responsibilities, his Shareholders Handbook (London: Effingham Wilson, 1884) and his other works consist of reproductions or paraphrases of the Companies Acts and other relevant legislation.

He did not hesitate to disapprove of legislation. The clause in Table A to the Companies Acts of 1862 permitting an auditor to be a member of the company was 'most extraordinary' (Lecture II, p.23). The Bankruptcy Act of 1883 (which provided for Official Receivers in the place of trustees appointed by the creditors, thus transferring much work away from professional accountants) could only be described, he thought, as a 'direct attack upon the profession' (Lecture VII, p.203). Indeed, although Pixley does not mention it, Robert Palmer Harding, second president of the ICAEW (1882-83), actually resigned his membership in order to accept appointment as Chief Official Receiver.

Pixley regarded legal knowledge as part of the higher education now required by accountants. Until about 1870 a knowledge of bookkeeping and an ability to analyse accounts had been all that was necessary, but, he argued, since then familiarity with the principles and practice of certain branches of law had become necessary. Later, some accountants were to cast economics in the same role.

Practice and theory

Pixley is at his best when describing the practical details of an accountant's work, especially where these involve the application of legal rules. Much of his writing displays those qualities of common sense, close attention to detail, and practical financial knowledge which have contributed so much to the growth of the accountancy profession. He differed from most of his contemporary accountants in his obvious enjoyment of writing.

Commonsense, attention to detail and practical financial knowledge came together best in a book such as Clubs and their Management (1916 and 1927). Contemporary readers must have benefited greatly from its advice. The modern reader can delight in the introductory chapter which describes how the supersession of the old-fashioned English cook by chefs educated in a Parisian kitchen; the coming of gas, electricity, telephones and lifts; the formation of the Metropolitan Water Board; and increased taxes had all combined to increase expenditure and to make good financial management all the more necessary. Pixley was a leading member of the Chartered Accountants' Dining Club.

Clubs and their Management includes a chapter on the duties of a librarian. Pixley was chairman of the Library Committee of the ICAEW for no less than forty years (1893-1933) and some, at least, of the credit for the Institute's fine collection must go to him. It was during his presidency that the first ICAEW Library Catalogue was published. He did not agree with the English Institute member who wrote to The Accountant of 6 January 1894 arguing that 'no professional work that is more than about twenty years old has any value save for archeological /sic/ purposes; and it would be a pity if any of the funds of the Institute were expended in fanciful directions while any practical work remains to be done'. This was a comment on a letter from Pixley (The Accountant, 16 December 1893) stating that the Library Committee of the Institute was 'very desirous of obtaining a complete collection of works on bookkeeping in every language'.

Pixley's writings are less convincing when they deal with matters of what we would now call financial accounting theory where he tends to make dogmatic statements without providing much in the way of justification. There are two examples in his 1904 Congress paper which he obviously prepared with much care. He discusses the depreciation of leasehold property and mentions that auditors trying to insist on depreciation throughout the life of the lease are frequently met with the argument, 'which in many cases is a perfectly correct one, more especially in a city like London, and other centres where property is gradually increasing in value, that a lease after many years is worth more than it was when originally purchased' (p.131). What should the auditor reply? Pixley does not tell us. Later he states that it is exceedingly difficult to make shareholders understand that 'the values placed against the items are merely those of the books, and that it does not necessarily mean that their commercial values in any way approach the figures set out'. It is difficult, he states, to explain to a meeting of shareholders (more particularly of a company that has gone into liquidation) that 'the assets are not expected to yield a quarter, or even a tenth part, of the amounts taken credit for in the last audited Balance Sheet of the company' (p.139). He leaves the argument at this point.

Pixley was not alone among the accounting pioneers in finding it difficult to explain _why_ accountants acted the way they did. Indeed, this is still one of the weaknesses of the accountancy profession.

Prudence and the going concern

Pixley's profession was one which, in the words of the historian of the Irish Institute, 'was born through bankruptcies, fed on failures and frauds, grew on liquidations and graduated through audits'. Many limited liability companies were dissolved almost as fast as they were formed. In the second half of the 19th century about one-quarter of companies were dissolved within three years of registration, about one-half within ten years and getting on for three-quarters within twenty years.

The succession of 19th century bank failures, notably those of Overend Gurney in 1866 and the City of Glasgow Bank in 1878, must have profoundly influenced men like Pixley with their City and financial connections. It should also be remembered that after the boom year of 1873 prices fell almost continuously until 1900.

It is not surprising then that Pixley's writings lay great stress on prudence and the continuity of the going concern.

This explains his approval of secret reserves: when such reserves were made bona fide in the interests of the company 'then - although the Auditors may consider them beyond what may be actually required - they are ... justified in passing them without comment, knowing that in so doing the financial position of the company will be strengthened' (Congress of Accountants, p.140). In the 1922 edition of Auditors (pp.537-539) he notes that arguments have arisen from time to time in financial reviews and newspapers as to the propriety of such reserves but in his view many companies had passed away which would probably still be in existence 'had they been provided with a Secret Reserve legitimately created'. He did not accept the objection that secret reserves deprive those who happen to be shareholders at the date of creation of or addition to such a reserve of participating in a higher dividend than that which was declared. In Pixley's view the directors should consider not the interests of individual shareholders or group of shareholders but the preservation of the capital of a company and its continued existence as a going concern. If, however, the auditor is satisfied that the secret reserves are being created not in the interests of the company but for other purposes, such as speculation in the company's shares, the auditor should state in his report that in his opinion the liabilities are exaggerated, or the assets undervalued, as the case may require.

The fact that such reserves were secret could, of course, lead to their abuse, but until the Royal Mail case of 1931 Pixley's views were widely held by auditors.

Pixley attempts no general theory of asset valuation and income measurement and is not at all explicit about accounting conventions, but insofar as it is possible at all to pull his statements into a coherent system, they appear to be a consequence of the emphasis he places upon prudence and the going concern. Preparing a company's accounts on the basis that it is a 'going concern' refers not to the amounts at which a company (or its net assets) could be bought or sold but to balance sheet values and resulting profit figures which would ensure as far as possible the continued existence of the enterprise.

It is the duty of the directors, wrote Pixley, to keep the capital of their company intact and to do their best to make it a permanent institution (Lecture II, p.35 and Auditors, 1922 ed., p.413). Their object 'ought not to be to pay as high a dividend as possible, but to do exactly the reverse. A percentage on the capital paid away in dividend can never be recalled, while one retained in hand is always available ... a director who consents to pay a quarter per cent more dividend than he is absolutely compelled is exceedingly foolish, and ... a secretary who assists him to do it is still more foolish ... thousands of companies registered since the Act of 1862 came into existence have been wound up ... through this insane craze of paying high dividends' (ibid, p.34 and p.412).

Profit is thus regarded as an indicator of the amount available for prudent distribution in cash dividends and is closely linked with increases and decreases in monetary assets. It is thus consistent for Pixley to argue both that 'All stocks should be taken at cost price, never above it, and where the stock has been for some time on hand, and has suffered from deterioration, or the market has depreciated since it was bought, a proportion ought to be written off for depreciation in this respect' (Lecture IV, p.80) and that, on the other hand, the auditor should not object to bank directors wishing to show their securities at market value although 'As a matter of prudence, however, he might suggest the cost being inserted in the Balance Sheet, supposing the securities have not depreciated in value, and it being stated, in a foot note, the actual market value at the date on which the Balance Sheet is made out' (Auditors, 1881 ed., pp.130-1, 1922 ed., p.503).

Increases and decreases in the market values of fixed assets are not considered relevant for a going concern which does not intend to sell such assets. Thus, whilst current assets should normally be written down to net realisable value where this is below cost, the going concern value of fixed assets 'has no relation whatever to current market value' which is too low. Pixley explains this as follows (by 'credit side' he means,as was normal at the time, the right hand or assets side of a British balance sheet):

> When the word 'value' is used in connection with the amount placed against any item on the credit side of a Balance Sheet, it must not be understood to represent what that item would realise if offered to sale in an open market. It represents what that item is believed to be worth to the concern or individual owning it, having regard to the fact that the owner is what is technically known as a 'going concern'.

For example, suppose a Company, firm or individual decides to erect a factory, selects as an eligible site a plot of freehold land near a railway station and after negotiation the site is acquired, naturally at a somewhat higher price than the surrounding land, having regard to the fact that it was a small portion specially selected out of a larger area belonging to the vendor. Having acquired the land the purchaser instructs an architect to prepare plans for the building, calls for tenders for construction of the factory and eventually has the factory built by a contractor. In the meantime designs and estimates are obtained from engineers for the particular class of machinery to be erected in the factory which after being specially made is installed. A large quantity of belting, workmen's tools and other sundries are necessarily purchased, and the factory commences operations.

In making up the Accounts for the first financial period, say about twelve or fifteen months after the commencement of business, the Directors of the Company or the partners of a firm, or the individual owning the concern, as the case may be, have to determine on the amount to be placed on the credit side of the Balance Sheet in respect of the land, the building, the plant and machinery, the belting, the furniture, fittings, and the loose tools of the workmen.

According to some of the theorists the only value to be placed on these items is the value the various classes of property would fetch in the open market. This would have the result of the land being valued as a small holding, the only purchaser of which, if offered for sale, would probably be the original vendor, who would be able to acquire it at a depreciated value. The building, which would probably be useless except as a factory, and, even if purchased as a factory, would have to be again refitted for manufacturing some other class of goods, or might have to be adapted for some totally different purpose, or perhaps even pulled down and the materials disposed of as second-hand building material, could only be valued at a much lower rate than the original cost. The plant and machinery, having regard to its position and the fact of its having been used, would certainly not be valued at above 50 per cent, of its cost, and under certain circumstances might only be valued as scrap iron - while the furniture would undoubtedly be subject to very heavy depreciation, as likewise the workmen's tools.

In other words, even taking a much more sanguine view of the valuation, a valuation on the basis of the theorists would necessarily be a very low one, and that value inserted in the Balance Sheet would probably show the concern insolvent on the preparation of its first Accounts.

On the other hand, if the anticipations of those who purchased the land, erected and fitted up the factory, have been fulfilled and the concern is likely to continue, the practice of preparing a Balance Sheet is to treat this property as being worth the cost price only subject to a certain allowance for what is known as 'depreciation', which is discussed elsewhere.

> In other words, the value placed upon the property and the assets, generally is the value of what it is worth to a 'going concern' and has no relation whatever to current or market values. Common sense must support this view and treat the theory of having assets at their actual value on the credit side of a Balance Sheet as impracticable. (Auditors, 1922 edition, pp.519-521)

As time went on it became clearer to Pixley that this approach did not lead to the balance sheet based on market values (net realisable values) that the lay reader might expect. The first edition of Auditors did not stress the 'technical' nature of balance sheets in the way that later ones did. A reference in 1881, for example, to a balance sheet showing the 'exact financial position of the Company' (p.129) became by 1922 the financial position 'as ascertained from the Books of Account' (p.518).

But if market fluctuations could be ignored, depreciation could not be. A company which distributed a 'profit' against which no charge had been made for depreciation would have difficulty in replacing its fixed assets and might soon cease to be a going concern.

Pixley refers on a number of occasions to the then common and, in his opinion, objectionable habit of companies deciding on the dividend and regarding any balance available as 'depreciation' (e.g. Lecture II, p.34 and Auditors, 1922 ed., pp.412). He is concerned that depreciation should be treated as an expense not an appropriation.

In a rather startling passage for the modern reader, Pixley states that it is a matter of no importance whether in the balance sheet the depreciation 'be deducted from the property account, or whether it be added to or form the commencement of a "reserve".' His only fear is that there is a temptation to transfer from a 'reserve' in order to pay a dividend which would not occur if the depreciation were written off the property account (Lecture IV, p.8). Such an attitude fits oddly with a desire to show unexpired historical costs but is consistent with an emphasis on prudence and the continuing existence of a going concern.

At times Pixley does appear to be arguing for an unexpired cost theory of asset valuation but the evidence is unclear. For example, chapter XII of Accountancy discusses 'the theory known amongst professional Accountants as that of "spreading expenditure".' When it is believed, he writes, that expenditure during the current year will have a beneficial effect on the Profit and Loss Accounts of the following years it is 'recognised as being a thoroughly sound commercial custom to "spread" this expenditure over a term of years' (p.253).

But he is at pains to point out that a balance of Preliminary Expenses on a balance sheet should be clearly set out so that it should not be mistaken for an asset. He does not state whether advertising carried forward is an asset or not but he does say 'there should only remain ... an amount representing advertising which it is believed will beneficially influence future business' (p.255).

Interests outside accounting

Pixley had a number of interests outside accounting. He was a Fellow of the Society of Antiquaries and the author of A History of the Baronetage (1900), a major work still regarded by authorities on the subject as of value, especially for its reprints of many documents not otherwise readily available. He was one of H.M. Lieutenants of the City of London and at one time Lieutenant-Colonel commanding the 1st Cadet Battalion of the King's Royal Rifle Corps. Later he was Treasurer of the Boy Scout Movement.

Pixley's contribution

What was Pixley's contribution to accounting? It is clear that he was not an original thinker of the calibre of Dicksee or de Paula. He is too often content to record practice in a rather uncritical way and without adequate explanation. The Accountant commented in its columns on a number of his lectures, usually praising his ability to set out clearly what was generally known, but criticising the lack of depth or originality (e.g. 4 July 1891; 3 June 1893).

His importance lies in his ability to reflect and write down current practice as it developed. He was a pioneer who helped to build up a new profession, to raise its educational standards and its standing in the community. He rightly saw that the future of the practising profession lay with auditing. What we would now regard as weaknesses: the restriction of the profession to middle class entrants, the disregard of some shareholder needs, the lack of a theoretical framework, were of less importance in his time. That the British accountancy profession has yet to shake itself free of them can hardly be held to be his fault. In the centenary year of the ICAEW he can be recognised as one of the pioneers who, for good or ill, brought the profession to where it is today. As the writer of the first textbook on auditing his name is not likely to be forgotten.

CHAPTER 4

JOHN MANGER FELLS, CBE, FSAA, FCWA, 1858-1925

Unlike our other five pioneers, John Manger Fells was an incorporated not a chartered accountant and indeed for much of his career should strictly be regarded as 'unqualified' or not an accountant at all. On his marriage certificate (1897) he calls himself a business organiser and he did not become a member of the Society of Incorporated Accountants and Auditors (established 1885) until January 1902 although he was later to become a member of its Council and one of its examiners. He also became a fellow of the Institute of Cost and Works Accountants (now the Institute of Cost and Management Accountants) which was established in 1919, six years before Fells' death.

His claim to a place in this book depends mainly on his pioneering and highly successful work Factory Accounts, first published in 1887 during the period (1884-1889) when he was Accountant and Assistant Secretary of the Brush Electrical Engineering Co. (then known as the Anglo-American Brush Electric Light Corporation). His co-author was Emile Garcke (1856-1930), an electrical engineer associated with the same company from 1883 to 1893, eventually becoming its Chairman and Managing Director. Both were aged about 30 at the time of first publication. Factory Accounts was the leading English work on costing until the First World War.

Few details of Fells' early life are available. He was born in Deal, Kent, the son of a tailor and woollen draper, and educated at Deal College. He started his commercial career in the accounts office of a railway company. In 1889 he left Brush Electrical to join the Salt Union Ltd., first as Superintendent Accountant and later as General Manager. In 1899 he commenced practice in the City of London as a consulting accountant.

Fells was an expert witness in test cases before the Railway and Canal Commission Court, and at the time of his death was Consulting Accountant to the London Chamber of Commerce and the Associated British Chambers of Commerce on port and dock charges and railway rates. He was an original Fellow of the Royal Economic Society (founded in 1890 as the British Economic Association) and his writings show a greater knowledge of the economic thinking of his time than was usual among accountants. The leading English economist of the day, Alfred

Marshall, referred approvingly to Garcke and Fells' book in his Principles of Economics (1890) and his Industry and Trade (1919). Indeed, The Accountant in its review dated 5 May 1888 of the first edition of Factory Accounts went so far as to describe it, not very justly, as 'in the nature of a work on political economy'.

Fells married in 1897, his wife predeceasing him in 1918. There were three sons and one daughter of the marriage.

The costing renaissance

There could be no useful development of factory accounts until the development of factories themselves was sufficiently far advanced. Garcke and Fells begin their book with the following introductory comments:

> With the rapid development of the modern Factory System has arisen the need for regulations which would not have had application at a time when production was carried on with little, if any, industrial organization. The extent to which by the aid of machinery the specialization of labour is now carried, generally involves the passing of an article through as many hands or machines as there are processes in its production, and renders a further extension of routine and registration necessary. When artisans performed in their own dwellings and with their own hands, unassisted by steam or other motive power, all the operations necessary to the production of a complete article, the need for the regulation by statute of the periods and conditions of employment was not very obvious, whilst the most simple form of accountancy sufficed to ascertain the cost of an article thus produced. The establishment of large factories, however, where numbers of persons of both sexes co-operate through the division of labour in the production of articles of consumption, has changed the industrial conditions of society.
>
> Under these altered conditions employers find it economical to adopt methods of supervision and of registration which, prima facie, make production more costly. The advantages, however, of the combination of labour - of each workman confining himself to one process, and that always the one for which he is best fitted - are so great that the expenses of the necessary organization are insignificant in comparison. Experience has shown that wherever the magnitude of the operations renders it practicable, every further extension of this principle of specialisation results, in spite of the increased expense of administration, in an economic advantage. (4th ed. pp.1-2)

They also claim, with justification, to have written the earliest text on the subject. The factory system had been established in Britain long before

1887. Why had demand for a work on factory accounts not become apparent earlier?

It may be, of course, that accounting practice was well ahead of the text books and the researches of McKendrick into the costing records of Josiah Wedgewood in the late eighteenth century (Economic History Review, April 1970) and of Stone into the cost accounting system of Charlton Mills of Manchester, 1810-1889 (Accounting and Business Research, Winter 1973) demonstrate that this was certainly the case to some extent. On the other hand, it is probable, as Edwards argued in an article in The Accountant (vol. 97, 1937, p.283) that, in the engineering trades at least, in the first three-quarters of the nineteenth century business was so good that manufacturers had little need to pay attention to methods of costing.

By the time Garcke and Fells came to write, profit margins were declining and pricing was becoming more competitive. At the same time companies became more capital intensive and overheads became more important. As a result, the last three decades of the century were marked by what Solomons has described as a 'costing renaissance' (Studies in Cost Analysis, 1968, p.17)

'Factory Accounts'

Garcke and Fells' book Factory Accounts. Their Principles and Practice A Handbook for Accountants and Manufacturers was the work of the costing renaissance. The eight chapters of the first edition (1887) cover labour, stores, prime cost, stock, fixed capital and surveys. The appendices, which deal with such matters as the income tax acts, the rating of factories, the law relating to fire and boiler insurance and the factory and workshop acts, provide material covering most aspects of the environment of the contemporary manufacturer. As Wells has pointed out (Accounting and Business Research, Autumn 1977, p.300), the joint authorship of the book neatly combined the two professional groups which had the greatest interest in developing costing methods, and the most to gain from their introduction.

The fourth edition of 1893 does not differ substantially from the first; it was reprinted by the Arno Press in 1976 and is thus easily accessible to the modern reader. Page references in this chapter are to this edition except where otherwise stated. Later editions were considerably extended, the sixth edition of 1911, for example, containing more discussion of cost ledgers, indirect or incidental expenses and their allocation, depreciation, machinery use, subsidiary books, and methods of remunerating labour.

Garcke and Fells claimed with justification that theirs was the first attempt to place before English readers 'a systematised statement of the principles regulating Factory Accounts; and of the methods by which those principles can be put into practice and made to serve important purposes in the economy of manufacture' (p.v). They further claimed that the principles of such accounts 'do not differ in the main from those general rules on which all sound book-keeping is based, and we have but applied fundamental axioms to the practice of an important and extending branch of industrial accounts' (p.v). Cost accounts were integrated into the double-entry system.

The Accountant's reviewer of the first edition was not convinced:

> ... our impression of it is that it is more of a theoretical than a practical work. It does not purport to deal with the ordinary financial books. It is rather concerned with the wages and time books, stock books, and matters of a similar nature, which, as a rule, do not come within the scope of an accountant's duties. (The Accountant, 5 May 1888, p.278)

The Accountant was right in the sense that most practising accountants of the period had very little contact with manufacturing organisations, even in their audit work. Their clients were mainly engaged in banking, insurance, railways, water, docks and mines. The Accountant, as Fells put it later, tended to present 'the average mind of the profession' (The Incorporated Accountants' Journal, December 1910, p.69). It was inclined to disapprove, on behalf of the accountancy profession, of things which it did not quite understand.

Accounting for stores and stock

The Accountant's reviewer singled out for adverse comment Garcke and Fells' claim that:

> It is not too much to say that for a manufacturing or trading concern to be well organized, the storekeeper or warehouseman should be able to state, by referring to his Stores or Stock ledgers, the actual quantities of any kind of material, or stock, on hand with the same facility and precision as the accountant can ascertain from the books the balances of cash at the bankers or the amount of securities in the safe. (p.5)

What accountant, the reviewer asks, would agree to these remarks - 'The ideal here sought after is simply unattainable in most cases.'

The way in which the ideal could be attained was set out in detail in Garcke and Fells' chapter on stores where specimen rulings are given of a stores requisition, a stores requisition book, an invoice register book, a stores ledger, an invoice endorsement, an instruction to foreman of works, a stores warrant, a stores issued book, a stores rejected book, a stores debit note and a shop returns book, plus a diagram showing the relation of the books and forms used in connection with stores.

Specimen rulings are a feature of Factory Accounts: there are 51 in the first edition, and 57 in the fourth and sixth.

Marginal costing

Garcke and Fells also consider the problems of stock valuation. They commend the practice adopted by the best manufacturing firms of valuing stores at the net cost or invoicing price to them and manufactured articles at their cost of production without any addition for profit, or for standing charges (establishment expenses) (p.122). By establishment expenses they meant those 'general expenses which cannot be directly charged to any particular process or branch of a business' (p.234).

In two interesting passages they argue that:

> The establishment expenses and interest on capital should not, however, in any case form part of the cost of production. There is no advantage in distributing these items over the various transactions or articles produced. They do not vary proportionately with the volume of business. A large increase in the value of orders received would not necessitate a like augmentation of the office staff, nor would a sudden and serious falling off in trade enable a firm to effect an immediate or proportionate reduction of general expenditure. The establishment charges are, in the aggregate, more or less constant, while the manufacturing costs fluctuate with the cost of labour and the price of material. To distribute the charges over the articles manufactured would, therefore, have the effect of disproportionately reducing the cost of production with every increase, and the reverse with every diminution, of business. Such a result is greatly to be deprecated, as tending neither to economy of management nor to accuracy in estimating for contracts. The principals of a business can always judge what percentage of gross profit upon cost is necessary to cover fixed establishment charges and interest on capital. (p.73)

> The practice of including in the valuation of Stock a percentage for establishment expenses or standing charges is one which cannot be too strongly condemned, if on no other ground than that a business which is really the reverse of profitable might, by the simple device of manufacturing and accumulating a large stock, be made to appear for a time as at any rate self-supporting. That is to say, a business might be made to appear flourishing, while as a matter of fact it is becoming less solvent, by reason of its cash and other available assets being converted into manufactured stock which may never be realizable, and by the standing charges (if these are included), which in the absence of bona-fide business transactions would represent losses, being made to figure in the balance-sheet as good assets in the shape of stock on hand. (p.122-3)

As Solomons has pointed out (Studies in Cost Analysis, p.34) Garcke and Fells oversimplify by identifying the distinction between establishment expenses and manufacturing costs with that between fixed and variable costs but he rightly counts them among the founders of the 'marginal cost' school of thought.

When W.J. Ashley of Birmingham University (one of the few leading economists of his day interested in business economics rather than political economy) pointed out that they seemed specifically to exclude establishment expenses and interest as items in the cost of production, they replied:

> We did not mean to convey that Establishment Expenses and Interest were not elements in the cost of production of the aggregate of the commodities manufactured. What we desired to point out was that, from the commercial standpoint of a manufacturer desirous under competitive conditions of obtaining business data on which he could act as to the price of the product, Establishment Expenses, and in some measure Interest, would not be regarded as items in the cost of production of particular commodities in so far as it regulates price. (italics added) (6th ed. p.93 n)

At a later point in Factory Accounts, Garcke and Fells point out that full advantage of the economies arising from the use of machinery is not likely to accrue until the principle of working double or treble shifts is more extensively adopted, since interest on capital and depreciation are largely independent of the number of hours employees work (p.140). Their discussion of piece work shows an appreciation of what would today be called the behavioural aspects. They support the idea of industrial partnership but realise the difficulties and suggest that if necessary a company's books could be inspected confidentially on the employees' behalf by a sworn accountant (pp.148-9).

Standard costing and scientific management

There is no mention of standard costing or the scientific management movement in Factory Accounts. These were American developments on which Garcke and Fells did not specifically comment. They do, however, include an appendix on Nomenclature of Machine Details by Oberlin Smith of the American Society of Mechanical Engineers and the following passage in their chapters on stores:

> Before any order to manufacture is given it is advisable, as tending to produce greater economy in cost of production, that the person best acquainted with its processes and details should estimate the probable cost to be incurred in wages and materials, in the production of the articles in question. This estimate should be a minimum rather than a maximum one, and the storekeeper having been furnished with particulars of it, should not without special authority issue more material for the order than is estimated. There is always a tendency for more time and material to be spent in manufacture than are absolutely necessary, and the probability is that when once a surplus quantity of material has been withdrawn from store, instead of being returned undiminished, it is in great part, if not entirely, lost in wasteful processes or in other ways; or the effectual localisation of cost may be hindered by foremen exchanging material with each other without the exchange being properly recorded. (pp.51-2)

Depreciation and distributable profit

Garcke and Fells were among the first to recognise the importance of Ewing Matheson's The Depreciation of Factories, Mines and Industrial Undertakings and their Valuation (first published in 1884; the second edition of 1893 was reprinted by the Arno Press in 1976) and they quote his views a number of times.

Matheson was an engineer who recognised the rise in importance of 'the profession of Accountant and Auditor' but was concerned that in matters of depreciation accountants 'must always be dependent for the accuracy of these data on those technically acquainted with the operations of manufacture'. In an introduction to the second edition of Matheson's book, William Charles Jackson, a member of the Council of the ICAEW, and in later years a partner of Pixley, pointed out that:

> ... Auditors, and especially those who have to deal with joint-stock or other concerns where the remuneration of the management is made wholly or partly dependent upon declared Profits, know in what various forms resistance to an adequate Charge against profits for Depreciation is presented.

> The fallacies underlying these objections present themselves again and again with the modifications caused by the lack of apprehension in some or the ingenuity of others. Mr. Matheson's work provides the Auditor with true antidotes to these fallacies, and it has been in past times used by the writer with satisfactory effect, where his own less-reasoned arguments have failed to convince.

Garcke and Fells' chapter in Factory Accounts on 'fixed capital' (i.e. fixed assets) begins with John Stuart Mills' definition of such assets as those which 'produce their effect, not by being parted with, but by being kept; and the efficiency of which is not exhausted by a single use' (Principles of Political Economy, Book I, ch.vi, par.1, 1848). They regard four factors as determining depreciation: cost; estimated life, extent and value of renovation or restoration; and residual value. In the sixth edition they interestingly add a fifth: 'Its value in use, or its present earning power, relatively and comparatively, to other instruments of production used for similar purposes' (p.100).

They do not recommend any particular method of depreciation but emphasise the importance of consistency. They are strongly against making depreciation dependent on fluctuations in the market prices of assets but conclude, with an echo of Guthrie's views on the subject, that 'A periodical survey of all buildings, plant etc., is, however, very important, and would serve, if no other purpose, as a very valuable check upon the system of calculating depreciation that may be adopted' (p.99). This conclusion leads them on to the question of how far a loss or profit on capital account, i.e. a diminution or increase in the realisable value of any of the assets, should affect the profit and loss account.

The first edition of Factory Accounts contains a lengthy quotation from the 1883 edition of Buckleys' The Law and Practice under the Companies Acts favouring treating capital account and revenue account as distinct accounts. Garcke and Fells conclude that:

> ... the practical view must be that, if at a given epoch the realisable value of all properties after liquidating all liabilities, is in excess of the amount of subscribed capital, such surplus constitutes profit, whether the gain has been made on capital account or revenue account; while the amount by which realisable assets fall short of the subscribed capital must be considered as loss. (1st ed., p.105)

Garcke and Fells went on to argue that so long as a business is a going concern (defined in their glossary as one the efficiency of which, for the purpose of profit, is maintained) it would probably be inadvisable for the profit and loss account to serve the purpose of an index of the fluctuations in the market value of the fixed assets essential to the carrying on of the business, for in such a case there would be an oscillation from a large profit one year to a large loss the next, although the nature, volume or lucrativeness of the current business may have remained without abnormal change. A sinking fund should be established to provide against eventual capital losses. Assets can be written up in value but the increase should be credited to a reserve.

These were matters which were to soon be considered by the Courts. The Neuchatel Asphalte Company case (1889) upheld Buckley's contention that capital account and revenue account were distinct accounts but Garcke and Fells did not change their views. In the sixth edition (1911) of Factory Accounts they were able to cite the list of cases, familiar now to most accountants, which followed in the 1890s.

Railway accounts

Fells started his career in the accounts office of a railway company and there are a number of references to railways in Factory Accounts. In the discussion on depreciation it is noted that:

> In some undertakings no cognizance is taken of depreciation in the accounts. In the case of most railways, for instance, the deterioration of the plant is taken to be adequately and fairly provided for by the current expenditure upon repairs and renewals which is debited to revenue account. This practice is defended on the ground that by the very nature of railway property the repairs and renewals must be at least equivalent to depreciation, and that an effectual check against any starving in maintenance is furnished by the certificates which the heads of the spending departments periodically give as to the conditions of the permanent way, plant, tools, buildings and rolling stocks. (pp.95-6)

They express some disapproval of this system, arguing that during the early years of a railway undertaking when expenditure for repairs, renewals and extensions is not so imperatively called for as after some years of working there is a danger that the profit and loss account will not be adequately debited with depreciation, and that even if it is, there is the risk of the accounts of particular years being prejudiced. The reference to 'extensions' as well as repairs and renewals seems to be a slip on their part. They also argue that the desire to maintain dividends and to show an average expenditure per mile may lead to only such work being done as will approximately cost the average amount.

In a discussion reported in The Incorporated Accountants' Journal of December 1901, Fells compared UK railway accounts unfavourably with those of US railways:

> Railway companies are proverbial sinners in respect to their accounts. Sir Joseph Pease was speaking some two or three months ago at a meeting of the North-Eastern Railway Company, and in the course of his remarks said that he had spoken to the accountant, to the goods manager, to the general manager, and to everybody else immediately concerned, and they were all agreed on one thing, viz, that they could no more 'spot' where the increase had arisen in the passenger traffic than they could 'spot' the decrease in the goods traffic. This is not at all a desirable state of things. It is very different from the manner in which the American railway companies' accounts are kept. Everybody knows that Mr. Pierpont Morgan, when he first took the railway companies of the United States in hand, gathered together and studied very exhaustively all the statistics he could get at, and as a result he pointed out that by the increase in rates or decrease in cost of one-tenth of a penny per ton per mile the companies would receive some £60,000 or £70,000 a year more. And if one looks at the elaborate accounts of these companies one can see what a great advantage these administrators have over administrators in this country. It may be asked, why should we endeavour to give people information for which they are not eager? Well, I take it that the province of an accountant is to make a man see all the various advantages that arise from a complete system of accounts, and if the accountants would only insist upon their clients being more accurate, with regard to what it has hitherto been the fashion to call subsidiary matters, but which are really matters of vital importance, it would undoubtedly open up a new era for accountants, and would also be of great service to manufacturers and traders.

Railway rates

'So important is the part played by British railways in the carrying on of our national commerce and industries' wrote Edwin A. Pratt in 1905 in his book Railways and their Rates (London: John Murray), 'that the question whether there is really any good foundation for the complaints which are made from time to time that the railway companies are more or less strangling that commerce and those industries by the imposition of excessive and unreasonable rates is one to which public attention may well be directed'.

The sixth edition of Factory Accounts (1911) explains that in view of the need that often arises of giving quotations for goods inclusive of free delivery, and of checking the rates charged by the railway companies, it is very desirable to record the quotations obtained, or rates paid, for freightage. The maximum tolls and charges for various classes of traffic over the various railways were prescribed in the Railway (Rates and Charges) Order Confirmation Acts passed in 1891 and 1892 consequent upon the Railway and Canal Traffic Act of 1888.

As a result of the Railway and Canal Traffic Act of 1894, railway companies could not increase their rates without public notice and could be called upon to justify any such increase before the Railway and Canal Commission Court. The interests of railway users ('traders') were looked after by the Mansion House Association on Railway and Canal Traffic.

Pratt, who was a supporter of the railway companies, argued that the result of the 1894 Act was that legislation which had been intended to safeguard the interests of the traders had deprived railway rates of flexibility which would have been of more practical advantage to them (Railways and their Rates, pp.27-8). Certainly, as was argued by Thomas Waghorn, a barrister who often appeared before the Railway and Canal Commission Court on behalf of the traders, the law became in practice 'complicated and intricate to the last degree' and upon many points 'unsettled and obscure' (The Law relating to Railway Traffic, London: Effingham Wilson, 1906, pp. 1, 4).

The most important of the cases dealing with increased rates were those of Rickett, Smith & Company, the South Yorkshire Coal Owners' Association, and Smith & Forrest. These three cases are discussed by Waghorn in his book and by Fells in a lecture on 'The Accountancy of To-morrow' delivered before the Incorporated Accountants' Students' Society of London, of which he was president, and printed in The Incorporated Accountants' Journal of December 1910.

In the Rickett, Smith & Company case (1895) the applicants accepted the railway companies statistics and did not even notice what Waghorn calls 'a flagrant miscalculation in the matter of waggon repairs amounting to about one-third of the whole alleged increase', although the error was picked up and commented upon by one of the Commissioners. South Yorkshire Coal Owners was the same case continued under a different name. The applicants engaged the services of a firm of chartered accountants to check the arithmetical accuracy of the railway company's bookkeeping. The arithmetic of the waggon repairs was put right but the company made countervailing corrections and the Court still remained only partially convinced as to the merits of the applicants' case.

In the Smith & Forrest case of 1899, the applicants were oil refiners, carrying on business at Manchester and Liverpool. The railway companies put forward the same accounts and statistical tables as before, stating that they had been used on previous occasions, and that they had come out 'unscathed and unchallengeable'.

Here is how Fells (the 'traders' accountant expert') described what happened next:

> An adjournment was obtained, the railway companies' statistics were dealt with by the traders' accountant expert, not as mere bookkeeping, but as applicable to the actual circumstances of railway traffic, and the Court was convinced, from the figures in the Midland Railway Company's own tables, that no increase at all was justified by them, or, as Mr. Waghorn describes it, the applicants shattered them (the statistics) to pieces before 'the Court and won their own case with the splintered fragments. This is probably the only case in which this has happened. Usually, especially when no very large sum is at issue, plaintiffs object to the cost of adjournment, and they object to the cost of expert examination, although they feel helpless at the vast array of figures marshalled against them. Possibly over half the traders' lost cases might have been won had the railway statistics been ordered to be presented before the hearing, and had they been submitted to expert examination before being admitted.' In Mr. Waghorn's opinion, if many of the cases traders have lost could be tried again and the accounts were tested in the same way as in the Smith & Forrest case, they would be found to have been lost through inability to grapple with the railway company's statistics. ('The Accountancy of To-morrow', Incorporated Accountants' Journal, December 1910, p.71)

The First World War

One of the incidental effects of the First World War was an increased emphasis on cost accounting. Delivering a lecture to the Institute of Industrial

Administration at the London School of Economics on 24 January 1922, with Sir William Plender in the chair, Fells explained how:

> In the course of hostilities during the war it was thought desirable for the State to assume control of a large number of industrial organisations in order to obtain munitions, foodstuffs, and other commodities requisite for the carrying on of the war, and also in connection with Governmental controls in relation to the maximum prices chargeable in the various branches of trade and for wholesale and retail transactions, and to adopt for this purpose systems of costing. (The Incorporated Accountants' Journal, February 1922, p.123)

In 1915 a Ministry of Munitions was created to take over from the War Office control of the production of anything required for war purposes. The new Ministry quickly became 'the biggest buying, importing, selling, manufacturing and distributing business in the world' (Sir Worthington Evans quoted by Sheila Marriner, 'The Ministry of Munitions 1915-19 and Government Accounting Procedures', Accounting and Business Research, Special Accounting History Issue, 1980). Its accounting procedures, however, owed little to books such as Factory Accounts. Cash accounting was used rather than accrual accounting, and the cost accounting techniques used left a lot to be desired. So, for that matter, did those of many of the Ministry's suppliers. In general, the needs and experience of the War did much to stimulate and encourage better cost accounting.

Like many other leading accountants, Fells was drawn into the war effort. The most important jobs went to younger men (Fells was by now in his late 50s) and to chartered accountants. Fells was appointed Private Secretary to the Surveyor-General of Supply, War Office and he was a member of several War Office committees including the Cost Accounting Committee. For these services he received a CBE (Civil) in 1920.

Fells was one of the supporters of the attempt to introduce accrual accounting and cost accounting into the British Army. His views on the subject are contained in an article entitled 'Cost Accounting and Rationed National Expenditure' published in The Cost Accountant of December 1921. The failure of the attempt, or rather the failure of the attempt to decentralise Army administration, has been chronicled by F.K. Wright in his paper 'The British Army Cost Accounting Experiment, 1919-25' in The Australian Accountant, November 1956.

Inflation accounting

Another effect of the War was to confront the accountancy profession for the first time with inflation. Prices more than doubled from 1914 to 1919. Fells was an early supporter of inflation accounting, writing in 1919 that 'it is absurd, of course, to compare the costs of to-day on a monetary standard with the cost of four or five years ago, and until the principle that has been urged so strongly by Professor Irving Fisher of stabilising monetary valuations is adopted, we ought to put in some co-efficients which show that £1 to-day is only the same thing as 10s four or five years ago'. ('Some Principles governing the Ascertainment of Cost', Incorporated Accountants' Journal, November 1919, p.34)

Fells did not develop his ideas further. Inflation was not a practical problem in the 1920s, when prices fell sharply back to the levels of before the War.

The Institute of Cost and Works Accountants

After the War cost accounting practitioners decided to form a professional body to encourage the development of cost accounting techniques, to hold examinations and to award qualifications. The existing bodies, to which many, but not all, of the cost accounting practitioners belonged made no provision for the acquisition of special skills in costing and took little interest in the subject. An Institute of Cost and Works Accountants (ICWA) was established in 1919, changing its name to the Institute of Cost and Management Accountants in 1972.

In 1922 the ICWA petitioned unsuccessfully for a Charter of Incorporation (such a charter was eventually granted in 1975). The petition was opposed by the chartered accountants and incorporated accountants, the council of the ICAEW arguing that cost and works accountants 'are not engaged in professional work, but are employed in the service of traders' (see The Accountant, 5 May 1923, p.683).

Fells became a Fellow of the ICWA and, as already noted, contributed an article to the 1921 volume of The Cost Accountant, the ICWA's journal established in that year.

Fells' contribution

Fells raised himself by ability and hard work from quite humble beginnings to a position of importance. Unlike the other pioneers in this book, he obtained his training and experience in industry and commerce. Factory Accounts triumphantly survived its initially lukewarm reception in the accountancy press, The Accountant pronouncing the sixth edition to be 'a reliable guide to all matters pertaining to factory accounts' (The Accountant, 22 July 1911, p.123) and the seventh and last as 'solidly based on principle' (The Accountant, 25 February 1922, p.281).

By the time Fells died in December 1925 cost accounting was beginning to achieve general recognition, as opposed to being the special interest of only a small number of innovative accountants and industrialists. Between the Wars leading qualified accountants in increasing numbers were following the lead of men like Francis D'Arcy Cooper and F.R.M. de Paula in moving 'out of the profession' into companies such as Unilever and Dunlop and demonstrating that good accounting was as essential for managers as it was for creditors and shareholders.

Fells did much to advance the profession and to dispel the image of the accountant as 'merely a man who can add up figures accurately, write a nice round hand, and who conforms to the regulations laid down by law in the conduct of his work, but beyond that ... is absolutely useless' ('The Accountancy of To-morrow', Incorporated Accountants' Journal, December 1910, p.73). As co-author of Factory Accounts Fells made a remarkable contribution. He deserves his place among the pioneers.

CHAPTER 5

LAWRENCE ROBERT DICKSEE, MCom, FCA, 1864-1932

Besides being the most prolific of the early writers on accounting, following the establishment of the new profession, Lawrence Robert Dicksee is distinguished among them in having been the first to carry his teaching into the universities.

Childhood and family background

Lawrence Dicksee was born in London in 1864 at 27, Howland Street, W. The house no longer stands, but its site is only a hundred yards or so from the present London School of Economics' Hall of Residence (Carr-Saunders Hall) in Fitzroy Street, adjacent to Fitzroy Square and two minutes' walk from the Post Office Tower. The Dicksees were a large, talented and united family of successful and distinguished artists. Lawrence's father, John Robert Dicksee (born in 1817) and his uncle, Thomas Francis Dicksee (born in 1820) lived and worked as artists in close association throughout their lives. They had shared premises in Soho in their twenties (at 36, Gerrard Street, and 53, Old Compton Street) and both had moved to Howland Street at or about the times of their marriages: Thomas first to No.23 Howland Street, and John later to No.27. John already had modest success and some reputation as a portrait painter, and Thomas was perhaps rather the more successful of the two as a painter and illustrator.

Thomas had four children at Howland Street, and John five, of whom Lawrence was the youngest. These nine children (six boys and three girls, all born between 1852 and 1864) must have made a lively group. The two households included other relatives from time to time and each had at least two domestic servants living on the premises. Both households later moved to Fitzroy Square (Thomas's to No.2 and John's to No.6) and when the children came in due course to set up house for themselves, they moved to addresses in the area of St. John's Wood and Hampstead and the close family associations seem to have continued.

In Lawrence's childhood, the families might have been described as at least 'of modest means' or 'comfortably off'. When the nine youngsters grew up they seem generally to have maintained and improved upon their parents' living standards and position. Most of the nine followed their fathers' professions in some field of art or architecture, with Lawrence's cousin Frank (who was eleven years his senior and had early success as a painter) shining the brightest.*

Possible influence of family environment on Dicksee's development

We do not know how it came about that with a family background rooted so firmly in the arts, Lawrence should have been launched into accountancy in 1881 at the age of 17. But he had been educated at the City of London School where his father had been teaching since 1852.ø John Robert Dicksee was also first curator of the City of London Corporation's works of art, and it may be that these links with the City, and the developments in accountancy then current, brought to notice the possibilities for Lawrence of a career in the new profession.

We can discern something of Lawrence's family environment in his work. His colleague and friend Stanley W. Rowland wrote at the time of Lawrence's death in 1932:

> He was intimate with few of his professional associates. To those few he revealed a man cast by nature for the life of an artist, although accounting translated his love of beauty into a desire for neatness and precision in all things ...
> (see The Accountant of 27 February 1932, p.284)

Certainly it was natural for a man with Lawrence Dicksee's background to turn readily to teaching. On the other hand, it is interesting to speculate whether the thought processes of the artist, with which Lawrence necessarily lived constantly during his formative years, may have worked against the full success of his important contribution to the development of accounting thought and ideas.

---

* Sir Francis Bernard (Frank) Dicksee: elected President of the Royal Academy (1924), knighted (1925), given the honorary degree of Doctor of Civil Law of Oxford University (1926) and created KCVO (1927). He was amongst many other things a Trustee of the British Museum and of the National Portrait Gallery. His death (in 1928, when he was 75) was followed by a splendid funeral service in Westminster Abbey, with representatives present from HM the King, the Prince of Wales, and other Royal personages, the Prime Minister and the Lord Mayor of London and a large congregation (British and foreign) of corresponding distinction.

ø John Robert Dicksee continued in his post as head drawing master at the City of London School until 1897, when he was already 80. He continued to paint, and exhibited his last picture at the Royal Academy's 1905 exhibition, a few months before his death. He was followed as head drawing master at the City of London School by his third son, Herbert, who at that time and for many years afterwards lived at Oak House, Kidderpore Avenue, Hampstead. When John Robert died in September 1905, his address was Platts Lane, Hampstead, where another son, Bernard, had a house at No.4.

Professor LAWRENCE R. DICKSEE, M.Com., F.C.A.

From *The Accountant*, 18 February 1922

Like most other early writers in the field, Lawrence Dicksee lacked formal training as a scholar, at any rate beyond school years, and though his consideration of accounting and accounting problems was extensive and deep, there is evidence that he lacked in some measure the stamina, determination, and power of analysis (to reject some inadequate conclusions and to persist in the elimination of some important loose ends) which might have been available to a mind of comparable quality well trained in the thought processes of science or the law.

Stanley Rowland, writing in love and admiration after Dicksee's death of his mode of working, said (in The Accountant of 27 February 1932):

> Dicksee's was a very remarkable brain. He had a power of rapid assimilation which gave him the material for confidence in his own knowledge. But he was able to pass everything through the processes of his own mind in such fashion that his teaching bore the impress of his individual minting. Consequently, he was rarely seen to consult other men's writings before delivering himself on any particular subject. For him the writing of an article was a matter for intense mental concentration, in course of which he called his forces to his command, and at the blast of his trumpet difficulties appeared to vanish. His dictating machine was his constant companion, and he could put into it long stretches of dictation which would transcribe with hardly the correction of a word.

Of course, the 'other men's writings' which Dicksee might have been more frequently 'seen to consult' were, at the time of his early work, sparse and often of indifferent quality. It was, indeed, Dicksee's strong independence of mind and his confidence in his own grasp of his subject which enabled him to play his important pioneering role in providing single-handed so large a portion of the accounting literature of his day. Inevitably, however, his lonely working style, in which writing followed swift on meditation, inclined him to miss (or to under-estimate) some invaluable references, occasionally in The Accountant in the years following his entry into articles, and later in some judicial opinions and judgements, the bases for which he might with advantage have weighed more patiently and assiduously.

1881-1892: Dicksee's early career

Lawrence Dicksee was conscious that, unlike many early leaders of the profession, he qualified by examination for membership of the Institute of Chartered Accountants in England and Wales. Following its incorporation by Royal Charter, the Institute had a membership in 1880 of rather under 600, including (to quote from Dicksee's Presidential Address to the Birmingham

Chartered Accountants' Students' Society in 1904) 'practically every practitioner worthy of ... serious attention.' (The Accountant, 19 November 1904, p.627). By the time Dicksee became an articled clerk in 1881 the membership had grown to nearly 1,200, about half having been admitted 'by virtue of their previous membership of existing Societies', and the remainder 'admitted by the Council'. (The Accountant, 10 June 1882, No.392, p.6). When Dicksee was admitted in 1886, there were about 1,400 members. (The Accountant, 7 May 1887, p.265). It may well be that Dicksee's early experience of the professional examinations was among the factors which awakened his interest in writing and teaching.

Dicksee's principal was George Norton Read, FCA (G.N. Read, Son & Co., chartered accountants, of 51, Queen Victoria Street, London, EC). He had been admitted to membership of the ICAEW in June 1880 and Lawrence Dicksee was his first articled pupil. There quickly came to be established between them the strong bond which Dicksee forged with a small number of his professional colleagues and friends. When Dicksee published his Auditing in 1892, it was 'affectionately dedicated' to G.N. Read.

After Dicksee's admission to membership of the Institute in November 1886, he set up in practice straight away, first at 6 Fitzroy Square, and later at 57, Moorgate Street, EC. However, his early venture into professional practice was 'only moderately successful' (The Accountant, 1 January 1921, p.3) and after three years Dicksee joined Mr. Peter Price in practice in Cardiff at 21, High Street under the style of Price & Dicksee. At the same time Mr. Price's elder son was articled to Dicksee.

Dicksee was to practise for five years in Cardiff. Price & Dicksee kept on Dicksee's London office for a time, but this did not attract sufficient business to justify its continuance. Dicksee was admitted to Fellowship of the ICAEW in November 1891. Three occurrences during his sojourn in Cardiff are notable: first, he began to work as a lecturer on book-keeping at the 'Technical Schools of the County Borough of Cardiff' as was to be stated, in due course, on the title page of Auditing; second, following a change of responsibilities resulting from Dicksee's entry into the partnership, a fraud was discovered in the accounts of the Cardiff Building Society of which Mr. Peter Price was Secretary; and third, Dicksee prepared and published in 1892 his first book, Auditing.

The building society fraud was a simple one, perpetrated over a period of years by a clerk with access to cash, and successfully concealed by him, despite recurrent audit by unqualified auditors. His main method for concealment (which called for some skill in timing and execution) was to alter individual mortgage account balances after they had been listed and checked by the auditors, but before they were added to provide the total for mortgage debtors. After the addition had been checked, the falsely inflated individual account balances were altered back again (with the 'total' left unchanged) so that any later references to individual balances would raise no suspicion. In all, the defalcations amounted to some £8,600 and the Building Society's directors and Mr. Peter Price made up the whole of the deficiency between them, with Mr. Price contributing

> nearly half of the total sum required (he giving up nearly the whole of his property), a fact the more remarkable as he was by no means a rich man or possessed of the means which some of the other officials could command. (from The South Wales Daily News quoted in The Accountant, 15 October 1892, p.776).

In 1890 frauds of the kind discovered at the Cardiff Building Society were common, and the Cardiff case received notice in The Accountant. The paper's readers were told in January 1890 that:

> It is the old tale of blind confidence in a clerk, and it is extremely doubtful whether the frauds would have been discovered even now, but for the fact of the Secretary having entered into a partnership which rendered the defaulter's services as his clerk unnecessary from that time ... (18 January 1890, p.28).

Subsequently, a correspondent asked for 'Details of the modus operandi', and on 19 April The Accountant published a long leading article (pp.193-195) in explanation, introduced as follows:

> ... we have been furnished with the recently issued accounts of the Cardiff Building Society, and also have been favoured with a detailed account of the mode by which the late clerk of the society managed to abstract a sum of nearly £8,600 before he was detected ...

The leading article recorded that 'Messrs. Read, Son & Co., of London' had been called in by the directors to make an independent investigation

> ... and from their report, which is a plain and concise statement of the work done, and the position of the Society, it is clear that the concern now stands on a sound basis ...

We may discern Lawrence Dicksee's hand in all this. The incident made a deep impression on him, as Auditing was to show. The Accountant had earlier noted (18 January 1890, p.28):

> ... there is not the slightest doubt that for an expenditure of a few guineas per annum for an audit by Chartered Accountants, /the amount of the defalcation/ would have been saved.

Peter Price was 65 when Dicksee joined him as a partner, and was well-known and respected in Cardiff for an unstinting, though unostentatious, contribution to public life in that City, particularly in relation to the establishment of the Cardiff Free Library. Price was a governor of the University College of South Wales and Monmouthshire in Cardiff, and was similarly associated with other organisations and also a magistrate. The shock and the heavy cost of the Building Society fraud was a severe blow to him. He died in 1892. Lawrence Dicksee carried on the Cardiff practice until 1894 when Price's son's articles were successfully completed. He then returned to London, and in September 1894 joined Arthur Sellars FCA in partnership at Copthall House, 48 Copthall Avenue, EC. Together they practised as Sellars, Dicksee and Co. Dicksee was to head the firm from 1898 until he died in 1932.

Marriage

Lawrence Dicksee took another important step in 1894. On 31 July at St. Andrews Church in St. Marylebone he married Nora Beatrice Plumbe, the daughter of an architect. The bride's 'residence at the time of marriage' was 13 Fitzroy Square. The couple lived for a while in Townshend Road, St. Johns Wood, and later in Antrim Mansions, Hampstead. Some time in 1908 or 1909 they moved to 153 Haverstock Hill, Hampstead, which was to be the family home for the rest of Dicksee's life. The house no longer stands. They had one child, a boy: he was a casualty of the 1914-18 war, and his death was a tragedy of particular poignancy for a man of Dicksee's warm and sensitive nature, the product of an environment in which children and family had had such importance*.

Dicksee's Auditing

Dicksee signed the preface to his first book _Auditing_ in Cardiff on 13 July 1892, and Gee & Co. published it later that year.[ø] Dicksee was 28. _Auditing_

---

* Dicksee's son was buried near Sunderland in County Durham. Dicksee's Will, made in 1925, includes the following:

> ... after my death my body shall be cremated or buried in the grave belonging to me wherein the body of my only son is buried and wherein my wife also desires ... /to/ ... be interred ...

ø The first edition of _Auditing_ was re-printed in 1976 by Arno Press of New York.

was well described by its sub-title as 'A Practical Manual for Auditors' and Dicksee placed his emphasis on identifying, elaborating, and explaining the methods to be adopted by auditors to achieve the objects of the audit, which he saw as

> The detection of fraud;
> The detection of technical errors; and
> The detection of errors in principle.

Dicksee also sought to consider and convey 'the leading principles that should guide an Auditor in the course of his investigations ...' and he aimed his work to a substantial degree at accountant students, while expressing in the Preface the hope that it would be 'also of some utility to practising members of the profession ... /especially/ when they find themselves face to face with the accounts of a business with which they have hitherto been unfamiliar'. For this latter purpose he included a long chapter on special considerations in different classes of audits. He regretted that lack of space had prevented 'a more full discussion of the various legal decisions that affect the duties and responsibilities of the profession'; in this, he was probably yielding to advice, as well as to inclination, since Pixley's Auditors ... already dealt substantially with such aspects. Dicksee nevertheless included two principal appendices, one comprising extracts, for reference, from a number of relevant statutes (mainly those dealing with corporate bodies registered otherwise than under the Companies Acts) and the other, extracts from Law Reports of decisions of interest to auditors. The extracts from statutes were similar to, though less extensive than, those provided in Pixley's book.

Dicksee's introductory chapter opened with a discussion of audit notebooks, instructions and programmes, the extent to which complete or test checking of transactions recording should be undertaken, and the rival merits of 'continuous' and 'completed' audits. There was an echo of the Cardiff Building Society incident in his reference to

> .. the extreme importance of completing each item of the audit as soon as possible after it is begun. Extensive frauds have escaped detection because the Auditor checked the balances of a Ledger one day, and the additions of such balances on the next - some of the items having been altered in the meantime. (page 10)

Auditing was an immediate success. Fourteen British editions were published during Dicksee's lifetime. The fifteenth was in preparation when he died. The book found a market also in the United States, and a first

'Authorized American Edition' was published in 1905. It was edited by Robert H. Montgomery, who had opened a New York office for the Philadelphia firm of Lybrand, Ross Bros. and Montgomery some while before. This first authorised American edition was re-printed by Arno Press of New York in 1976. Montgomery published his own Auditing Theory and Practice in 1912. It has been said that Montgomery's adaptation of Dicksee's text to American needs in 1905 marked the beginning of American literature in accounting. The American edition of 'Dicksee' was reprinted three times in 1907 and 1908. A second American edition was published in 1909.

Auditing was Dicksee's first, and also his most important, book. To those who read it in the late twentieth century, nearly ninety years after it was first drafted, it is most of all distinguished for a real attempt (in Chapter 5) to work out an acceptable and rational basis for asset valuation, depreciation, and income. For this, Dicksee recognised and considered the double-account system which had increasingly come into use during the nineteenth century, was prescribed under statutes of 1868 and 1871 for railway and gas companies, and was widely used for other similar undertakings such as docks and water companies. In placing so much emphasis on the double-account system, Dicksee was doing something which later writers felt no obligation to do, because in the years that followed the relative importance of the railways and the public utility undertakings diminished, and the double-account system became more and more archaic. It is a matter for much regret that Dicksee was not able to carry his discussion of value to a clear conclusion, though he returned to the problem in successive editions by adding further paragraphs. While we must regret that Dicksee failed to grapple adequately with the difficult concepts of value and income, we need to remember that we ourselves are still wrestling with them. Present problems can hardly be laid at Dicksee's door.*

Other publications

Even before Lawrence Dicksee left his Cardiff practice he was delivering occasional lectures to Chartered Accountants' Students' Societies in London, Leeds and elsewhere. After his return to London in 1894, these activities

* For a fuller consideration of Dicksee's ideas on value and income see J. Kitchen, 'Lawrence Dicksee, depreciation, and the double-account system' in H.C. Edey and B.S. Yamey (eds) Debits, Credits, Finance and Profits, Sweet and Maxwell, London 1974, 109-130; and J. Kitchen, 'Fixed asset values: ideas on depreciation 1892-1914' Accounting and Business Research, Autumn 1979, pp.281-291.

multiplied and he produced a steady output of lectures, articles and unsigned contributions to periodicals including The Accountant.

Besides Auditing, Dicksee's publications included Bookkeeping for Accountant Students in 1893, which ran to 8 editions during Dicksee's lifetime; Comparative Depreciation Tables in 1895 (3 editions to 1925); Bookkeeping for Company Secretaries in 1897 (6 editions during Dicksee's lifetime); and Goodwill and its Treatment in accounts also in 1897 with Frank Tillyard (4 editions before Dicksee died); Bookkeeping Exercises for Accountant Students in 1899 (4 editions during Dicksee's lifetime); Auctioneers' Accounts in 1901; Gas Accounts and Solicitors' Accounts both in 1902 and Depreciation, Reserves and Reserve Funds in 1903 (5 editions during Dicksee's lifetime). Dicksee also published Advanced Accounting in 1903, an important book, associated with his university courses at Birmingham and London, which ran to 7 editions during his lifetime.

Dicksee wrote several other small books on accounts for different classes of organisations, including Hotel Accounts (1905), Mines Accounting and Management (1914) and Garage Accounts (1929). He also developed an interest in business organisation, and Longmans Green brought out a book for him with that title in New York in 1910. Dicksee published Business Methods and the War (1915); Office Machinery, a handbook for progressive office managers (1917) which ran to 3 editions by 1928; and The True Basis of Efficiency (1922), part of a series for the London School of Economics edited by Sir William Beveridge and Professor A.J. Sergeant. Earlier, with H.E. Blair (Sir Herbert Blair) he had published a book on Office Organization and Management which was already in its third edition by 1914 and continued to appear in successive editions into the 1950s. If we take his published lectures and articles into account, it is not unfair to say that he provided a literature for accounting single-handed.

In 1932, The Accountant's obituary for Dicksee (20 February 1932, p.236) recorded that 'for nearly thirty years he [had been] a constant and most valued contributor to our columns' adding that Dicksee had been 'obliged through pressure of work to give up writing regularly for us' about eleven years previously. Stanley Rowland in his own obituary article for Dicksee (The Accountant, 27 February 1932, p.283) noted that 'There must be thousands of columns of The Accountant where those with eyes to see can detect the authentic and confident note of his style'.

We need to bear in mind the work involved in Dicksee's output of published material, and the labour of revision for later editions of his books, along with his part-time university teaching at London and (to 1906) at Birmingham; and we need to recall that throughout he continued to lecture outside the university, and (with everything) to fulfil the role of senior partner in a sizable accountancy practice. The load he carried was a formidable one.

University teaching

Lawrence Dicksee was appointed to the Chair of Accounting at the University of Birmingham in 1902, the first appointment to such a Chair in any British university. He was to become the first holder of a Chair of Accounting in the University of London, and he was also to be the first teacher of Accounting at the London School of Economics.

After his return from Cardiff, Dicksee had run the coaching classes of the London Chartered Accountants' Students' Society. The University of Birmingham announced in 1901 that they proposed to set up a Faculty of Commerce and they advertised a part-time Chair of Accounting. The advertisement appeared in The Accountant of 21 June 1902. The part-time post was to carry a stipend of £300 a year - from the third year. Because the duties in the first and second years would be 'comparatively light', the stipends for those years were set at £150 and £225 respectively. Dicksee's appointment was announced in The Accountant of 2 August 1902 with the following comment:

> Professor Dicksee's name will be so well known to our readers that it is unnecessary for us to enlarge here upon his qualifications for this important post. He has been one of the largest contributors to the literature of the profession, and the value of his works is shown by the fact that they are not merely sold extensively wherever the English language is spoken but are also in demand upon the Continent. Readers of The Accountant to which paper he has been a frequent contributor will regret the necessary severance of his connection. It is his intention to continue his practice in London, however.

A few months later, when the London School of Economics issued its sessional programme for 1902/03 it included an optional course of sixty lectures over two years on 'Accountancy and Business Methods' for the London BSc(Econ). Dicksee was named as the lecturer. He was to teach at LSE (always on a part-time basis) for the next twenty-five years.

Dicksee continued to live in London and he limited his visits to Birmingham to one day a week during term time, though his work for the Birmingham courses occupied much of his time. The MCom which he was awarded at the Birmingham Degree Congregation in 1903 seems to have been granted in recognition of his published work and his membership of Senate.

In 1906 Dicksee found it necessary to resign the Birmingham appointment in order to give more time to his work at LSE, which had been increased following the introduction there in 1906/07 of the so-called annual 'Army Class', a War Office scheme for the training in Business Methods and Business Administration of a limited number of serving officers, which ran successfully for many years. Dicksee was made Reader in Accounting in 1912, and given the title of Professor of Accounting and Business Organization in 1914. This title he held to 1919, when the London Commerce Degree was introduced and he was appointed to one of the newly established Chairs as Sir Ernest Cassel Professor of Accounting and Business Methods in the University of London.

Dicksee was Dean of the Faculty of Economics in the University of London in 1925/26. He retired in 1926 and was awarded the title of Emeritus Professor of Accountancy and Business Methods in the University in recognition of his work. He continued to give occasional lectures at LSE for another year or so, and to lecture elsewhere and to write into the last months of his life.

Published balance sheets and accounts

Under this title, Lawrence Dicksee gave an important public lecture at the London School of Economics on 7 October 1920. It was one of a short series of public lectures given at the School by the newly appointed occupants of the Sir Ernest Cassel Chairs. The lecture is notable because Dicksee took the opportunity to declare his position on secret reserves and what were sometimes called 'condensed balance sheets'. Dicksee said inter alia:

> Shareholders, in the nature of things, ... prefer uniform dividends. They are ... willing that distributions out of profits should ... increase, but they are ... inclined to be disappointed, ... when the rate of dividend falls. Accordingly, those ... responsible for the preparation of accounts, and for the successful conduct of a business, very naturally adopt in the main a procedure that tends in the direction of avoiding large distributions of profits which they know it will be impossible to maintain in the future. ... /A/ccordingly, we commonly find that where the dividend ... proposed ... is markedly less than the amount of the ... profits available to be divided, pressure is brought to bear by the shareholders for the dividend to be increased, and directors as a rule endeavour to resist that pressure where in their opinion the standard of distribution proposed is too high to be maintained. To assist them in resisting that pressure, it is a very common thing to transfer a ... part of the profits actually earned to a reserve, thus reducing the amount of undivided profits shown ...

Dicksee continued:

> Instead of transferring profits to a reserve that is clearly shown upon the face of the balance sheet ... the practice has grown up, and during recent years appears to be decidedly upon the increase, of piling up what are sometimes called 'internal reserves', sometimes 'undisclosed reserves', and sometimes 'secret reserves'. The term 'secret reserve' does not seem to be much used save by those who oppose this particular kind of policy and regard it as being highly undesirable.
>
> The effect of the policy is to withhold from those to whom the balance sheet may be sent the fact that the undertaking has made certain profits which have not yet been divided. The directors do not 'account' to the extent of such reserves. On the face of it that might seem to be entirely improper and highly unjustifiable, but it has been held that there is nothing whatever illegal about such a practice so long as it is not contrary to the regulations of that particular company.

Dicksee complained of the burden falling on the auditor required to decide whether he should make disclosure to the shareholders, and where he did not, to satisfy himself that the directors were acting in good faith for the benefit of the company and the shareholders.

Dicksee added:

> We cannot, and ought not to, complain, but rather to congratulate /the directors/ if their general policy is always to be on the safe side, and to aim at disclosing a position in their published balance sheets that is certainly not better than the true position. ... In spite of all this we must draw the line somewhere, or we shall find that we are driven to the conclusion that the balance sheet may mean little or nothing ...

Dicksee followed these remarks with a reference to a shipping company 'having total assets amounting to £1,305,000 odd' which explained '£1,073,811 of that amount ... simply ... as:

> Stock in steamships and investments, book value at 31 December 1918, after deducting depreciation previously written off.

Dicksee continued:

> At the annual meeting ... the chairman was asked whether he would state how much of that figure represented steamships and how much represented investments, and he said that it was not in the interests of the company to give that information. At that time, the £10 shares of the company stood at about £45. A little later the ships were sold and the company was wound up, and the return to the shareholders is now expected to be about £130 per share. One wonders whether it really was in the interests of the company that shareholders should have no information which would suggest to them that their shares were worth a very great deal more than the current market price.

Dicksee also complained of another practice, which was common in 1920, and which continued to be widely followed through the 1930s, of 'condensing' information on asset holdings by grouping together a number of items under one head, thereby disclosing and at the same time concealing information. Dicksee observed:

> The balance sheet should show in reasonable detail the grouping of its assets. Most balance sheets do that. Some certainly do not; and as an illustration of one that does not, I should like to read you an extract from a balance sheet of a well-known company. Explaining an outlay of upwards of $5\frac{3}{4}$ millions sterling, it does it in five lines of print, as follows: 'By land, water rights, reservoirs, effluent works, buildings, plant, machinery, office furniture, goodwill, designs, engraving, and sampling, as per last account, £5,776,212 19s. 8d. Further capital expenditure at cost (less sales) for the two years ended 26th June 1920, £14,922 16s. 11d.', making a total of £5,791,135 16s. 7d. I suggest that that is not an ideal way of disclosing to interested parties what the main resources of the undertaking consist of.

The experience of the 1920s and 1930s was to show that there would be no real advance in the standard of disclosure in the published accounts of companies until the setting-up and use of secret reserves had ceased to command the wide approval of businessmen. For this the necessary change of attitudes had to await the catalyst of the Kylsant case.

Dicksee's contribution

In his day, Lawrence Dicksee's contribution to education and ideas in accounting was an enormous one. And he won affection as well as reputation. There is a genuine ring about Stanley Rowland's introductory sentences in the Preface to the fifteenth edition of Auditing, which had been in preparation in the last months of Dicksee's life and was published soon after his death:

> Since the fourteenth edition of this work was published its distinguished author has been removed by death. The profession has lost a man of very singular ability, and I have been deprived of teacher, partner, and friend.

CHAPTER 6

SIR ARTHUR EDWIN CUTFORTH, CBE, FCA, 1881-1958

Arthur Cutforth was born in 1881, the year in which Dicksee entered articles with G.N. Read, and Pixley published his Auditors, their Duties and Responsibilities. Cutforth had something in common with Pixley, in that he aspired to and reached the highest levels in his chosen profession, and at the same time won early recognition as an author. Cutforth's Audits was published by Gee & Co. in 1906 when he was still aged only 25. It ran to a third edition by 1914, and the ninth edition appeared in 1936, when Cutforth was completing his second year as President of the Institute of Chartered Accountants in England and Wales (ICAEW), two years before a failure in health forced him to retire at the early age of 57.

Cutforth died on 7 April 1958 and The Accountant of 12 April noted the fact 'with deep regret', adding that the news had been received as their issue went to press, and that a more detailed notice would appear the following week. In its issue for 19 April 1958, The Accountant included an obituary note on Cutforth, written by Sir Russell Kettle, for many years senior partner of Deloitte, Plender, Griffiths & Co. and President in 1949-50 of the ICAEW.

When we remember that Cutforth had retired from Deloittes nearly twenty years before, Sir Russell Kettle's note is immediately impressive in the detail of its review of Arthur Cutforth's contribution and qualities as a colleague and partner, and of his interests and personality as a man. In that sense, the obituary Sir Russell Kettle wrote for Cutforth is exceptional: but Sir Arthur Cutforth was an exceptional man. We cannot more effectively begin this Chapter than by quoting what Sir Russell Kettle had to say about him:

> Nearly twenty years have passed since ill health brought to an untimely end Arthur Cutforth's professional life, but there must be many of his day and generation to whom the brief announcement of his death in your last issue recalls memories of a loyal and warm-hearted friend unspoilt by success.
>
> Arthur Cutforth served his articles with the late Mr. William Cash and after qualifying joined the staff of Messrs. Deloitte, Plender, Griffiths & Co.: his exceptional ability and engaging personality soon marked him out as a future partner and he was admitted a member of the firm in 1912. He quickly won a high reputation in the profession and took a leading part in the activities of the Institute of which he was President from 1934 to 1936.

Mr. ARTHUR E. CUTFORTH F.C.A.

From *The Accountant*, 18 March 1922

> Throughout /Cutforth's/ active life he was assiduous in furthering the interests of the younger members and students and his lectures and addresses on a wide variety of professional topics were notable for their lucidity and the ease with which practice and theory were harmonized. His contributions to the literature of the profession included well-known and authoritative works, such as Methods of Amalgamation and the Valuation of Businesses, Public Companies and the Investor and Audits. In the later years of his retirement he wrote a small volume of Random Reminiscences in which he recalled, in a very amusing manner, some of the lighter episodes of his professional career.
>
> In the field of public service Arthur Cutforth's business experience and organizing ability were utilised by successive Governments. He was Accountant Assessor to the Royal Commission on the Coal Industry in 1925; a member of the Food Council in 1932-38; Chairman of a Commission appointed to report on the reorganization of the Milk Marketing Schemes in Great Britain in 1935; a member of a sub-committee of the Committee of Imperial Defence concerned with the extraction of oil from coal in 1937 and a member of the Tithe Redemption Commission until 1938. He was High Sheriff of Hertfordshire in 1937-38. He was created CBE in 1926 and knighted in 1938.
>
> Arthur Cutforth was the trusted confidant and adviser of many clients who were attracted to him by his high qualities as an accountant, by his keen intelligence and by his personality and character. He brought to bear on his work an agile mind and a balanced judgement and his views, characterized by candour and fairness, commanded respect. His enforced retirement in 1938 was a severe blow to his firm, and a very real sense of personal loss was felt by his partners and the staff at 5 London Wall Buildings.
>
> In his younger days Arthur Cutforth was a keen mountaineer, both in Switzerland and in his beloved Lake District, and he was no mean cricketer; he regarded playing the first ball of an over from F.R. Spofforth, the Australian 'demon' bowler, as one of the most anxious moments in his life. He was an accomplished pianist and knew the music and words of Gilbert & Sullivan's operas almost by heart. And his friends will not forget his Puckish sense of humour.

Family background

Arthur Edwin Cutforth was born on 25 August 1881, at 34, Woodford Green, Woodford, Essex. When his father, Samuel Cutforth, registered the birth, he described himself as a Draper. Arthur's mother was Annie Maria Cutforth (nee Holland). There were two other sons of the marriage. Samuel Cutforth of Woodford Green appears (as tailor and draper) in the London Post Office Suburban Directory of 1880, but at that time he probably had not long traded there, for the previous issue (1876) contains no entry for a Cutforth. In successive editions of the same Directory from 1900-1928, Samuel Cutforth is recorded as of 'Ashlyn', Woodford Green, Linen and Woollen Draper. We may judge that he was in a good way of business, for when he died in 1931 at the age of 79, his effects registered at probate amounted to £69,659, a substantial fortune in those days.

The Cutforths had come from Lincolnshire. Samuel had been born on 29 October 1851 in Sutterton, Kirton-in-Holland near Boston. His father, John Cutforth, was a farmer, born nearby at Orby, whom the 1851 Census records as of Fosdyke Road, Sutterton, aged 44 with 40 acres and cattle and with the occupation also of 'salesman'. John's wife, Mary Anne (nee Odling) was eight years younger than her husband and aged 36 when Samuel joined the household which consisted (in 1851) of three daughters and three other sons, Mary Anne's mother, two (female) house servants and two (male) farm servants. By 1861, the Cutforth farm had grown to 153 acres, and four men were employed, as well as three house servants, including a groom and a dairymaid. Ten years later, the 1871 Census recorded no Cutforths at Sutterton.

Arthur Cutforth was educated at Bancroft's School, Woodford, and at Trent College, Derbyshire. His love for the Lake District, to which Sir Russell Kettle referred, was reflected in his marriage in 1920 (when he was 38) to Alizon Margaret Farrer Ecroyd, fourteen years his junior, and daughter of William Farrer, of Whitbarrow Lodge, Witherslack, near Grange-over-Sands. In later years, there was a second home at High Craig, Sawrey, Ambleside, and Ambleside was Cutforth's registered address at the ICAEW to which the Council's minute of 7 May 1958 referred when that body recorded with regret the report of his death, noting that he had been a Member of the Council from 1923 until 1940, and President from 1934 to 1936. Sir Arthur Cutforth had died in York, at 'The Retreat', a registered Nursing Home for the treatment of psychiatric illness founded in the late 18th century and run by the Religious Society of Friends.

In London, the Cutforths lived for many years (from about the time of their marriage) at St. James's Court, Buckingham Gate, SW1. Lady Cutforth survived her husband. There were three sons and a daughter of the marriage.

Cutforth's early days in the profession

Arthur Cutforth was articled to William Cash of Cash, Stone & Co. at the turn of the century, and took his Institute Examinations in June 1902 and June

1905. In each he was amongst those listed 'in order of merit', sharing eleventh place in the Final Examination (out of 100 successful candidates). When, after qualifying, he moved to Deloittes, Lord Plender (then plain William Plender) was already senior partner. Cutforth's professional career was to follow, in an important degree, in the footsteps of his principal and of William Plender.

William Cash came of a Quaker family and was the second of his name to serve as a partner in Cash, Stone & Co. The earlier William Cash had been one of the original members of the Council of the ICAEW in 1880, named in the Royal Charter. His son, Cutforth's principal, had been a member of the Chartered Accountants' Students' Society of London (CASSL) in its earliest days, and had held the position of Chairman of its Committee, taking a keen interest in its activities and delivering lectures to the Society from time to time. In 1938 he was to follow Lord Plender as President of the CASSL.

William Cash was to become President of the ICAEW in 1921. When his father had died in 1891, his seat on the ICAEW's Council had been taken by his partner William Alfred Stone. He, in turn, had retired from the Council in 1908, and William Cash had been elected in his place. He was to serve on the Council continuously to the time of his election as President and thereafter to 1940. William Cash took a great interest in the formation in 1921 of the London Members' Committee (fore-runner of the London District Society) of which he was the first Chairman.

The Accountant's article (2 July 1921) on William Cash, following his election to the Presidency, gave the above information amongst other things, and noted that Cash had served on a number of Committees and had acted from time to time as an Examiner for the Institute. *The Accountant* referred to various aspects of his work during the Great War as a member of the Board of Audit Control, to the evidence he had given on behalf of the ICAEW before the Royal Commission on Income Tax, and also before the Treasury Committee on the Audit of Exchequer Grants to Local Authorities. The two final paragraphs from *The Accountant*'s article are worth quoting for further indications of a long-standing interest in the governance and development of the profession, in the education and training of its students, and in work in relation to public utilities and local and national government in which Arthur Cutforth was to follow Cash, and (more) to follow Plender. *The Accountant*'s article on William Cash concluded:

> During the war Mr. Cash held various appointments, being one of the Referees appointed under the Munitions Act, 1915, and he is also a member of the Flour Mills Tribunal. He acted under Sir William Plender, the Controller, as Supervisor of one of the German Banks ...
> In addition to a general practice, Mr. Cash has specialised in questions relating to the Accounts of Gas and Water Companies and Local Authorities, and has been very largely engaged in giving evidence before Select Committees in both Houses of Parliament, being a familiar figure in the corridors at Westminster on these and kindred matters arising out of private Bills. He is a Director of several Gas Companies.

William Cash was to be a member of the Greene Committee on Company Law Amendment which was set up in 1925 and reported in 1926. Cutforth's career reflected the influence of his principal.

This is not the place to attempt more than a few words on Lord Plender, but there was much about him which must have impressed and influenced the young Arthur Cutforth. William Plender was twenty years older than Cutforth, and in his middle-forties when Cutforth went to work at Deloittes. The History of the Institute of Chartered Accountants in England and Wales and its founder bodies: 1870-1965 records (p.253) his 'modest beginnings as the son of a grocer and draper near Newcastle-upon-Tyne ...'. He was educated at The Royal Grammar School, Newcastle. At his death in 1946, Plender's entry in Who's Who said simply of his work at Deloittes 'Senior partner since 1904 of Deloitte, Plender, Griffiths & Co., London ...'. The ICAEW History refers to his Presidency on three occasions (1910-11; 1911-12; and 1929-30) and adds,

> ... his public services were prodigious as evidenced by the phenomenal number of Royal Commissions, Government and other committees and enquiries relating to financial, industrial, scholastic and charitable matters upon which he was invited to serve ...

Plender was knighted in 1911, created GBE in 1918, raised to the Baronetcy in 1923, and to the peerage in 1931. Amongst other things, he became High Sheriff of the Counties of Kent and London. Who Was Who (1941-1950) refers to some areas of his work which we may guess were of particular interest to Cutforth, e.g.,

> ... acted for the Metropolitan Water Board on acquisition in 1908 of London Water Companies; advised the Government in connection with the Port of London Bill, 1908; President, Chartered Accountants' Students' Society of London, 1909-38; ... Member, Royal Commission on Railways, 1913; ... Commissioner (unpaid) Railways Amalgamation Tribunal, 1921; First Independent Chairman (unpaid) National Board for the Coal Industry, 1921-25; ... etc.

Cutforth was admitted to a partnership in Deloittes in 1912. His Audits was already a couple of years into its second edition and selling steadily. He had two little books (on revision and general advice for examinees, to which we refer below) on Gee & Co.'s list from 1906 and 1908. He had given a major lecture in 1910 to the Sheffield Chartered Accountants' Students' Society on 'The Treatment of Fluctuating Currency in the Accounts of English Companies' (The Accountant, 19 November 1920, pp.690-699). In 1912, Arthur Cutforth was 31 and well launched on his career.

Students and accounting education

Cutforth gave early evidence of his interest in the education of articled clerks and their preparation for the Institute's examinations which he was to maintain throughout his professional life. In 1906, the year after his own admission to ICAEW as Associate, Gee & Co. published at 2/6d his Early Stages of Preparation for the Accountancy Papers of the Intermediate, a 100-page booklet of notes and explanatory material for subjects 'on which questions have been most frequently set in past Examinations'. There was liberal provision of simple examples, with past Questions at the end of each chapter. The booklet continued in Gee & Co.'s lists at least up to and after the outbreak of war. A smaller booklet of notes and advice (mainly in law subjects) appeared in 1908 at 1/6d with the title: The Month before the Chartered Accountants' Examinations: How to prepare, etc.

In 1906, however, Cutforth's main publication was the first edition of his Audits which Gee and Co. priced at 5/- 'to bring it within the means of the most needy student'. At that time, Dicksee's Auditing and Pixley's Auditors were acquiring the status of standard reference works. Dicksee's book was £1-1-0, not a small sum in those days. The Cutforth book was designed to set out the main principles of auditing and the practice of auditors in summarised form, and to present the information in a form suited to the requirements of students for examinations. It included a chapter in which representative Examination questions were set out, and in some cases answered and discussed. At about 200 pages, Cutforth's Audits was a clearly written and valuable summary work. It was not a 'cram' book, but the material was briefly set out with the main points developed briskly and shortly.

Cutforth did not wrestle with asset valuation and depreciation as did Dicksee. Audits included four pages on depreciation methods, two pages on the characteristics and operation of the Double-Account System, and four pages devoted to an example of the accounts of a Railway Company (among a dozen and a half similar examples of accounts of various classes of undertakings). But reference was also made in a Chapter on Special Features in Various Classes of Audits, to the relation of the Double-Account System to audits of Railway, Gas, Water, Electric Light and similar companies. Cutforth's book did not include the extracts from Statutes and Reports of decided cases which added to the bulk of Pixley's Auditors, and more particularly of Dicksee's work. Dicksee's Auditing held its price for the time being, but Cutforth certainly found a market for Audits, as we may judge from the fact that Dicksee's ninth edition, published in 1912, was priced at 10/6d, although it ran to more than 1,000 pages. Cutforth's second edition appeared in 1910 (200 pp.), and the third in 1914 (238 pp.). The book's popularity was established. Three further editions had appeared by the mid-'20s, and three more by the mid-'30s before Cutforth retired.

A particularly interesting example of Cutforth's involvement with students and his concern for education for the profession was his lecture in 1912 to the CASSL with the title: 'Can the Institute Examinations be improved upon?' (reprinted in The Accountant of 8 June 1912). He introduced his subject with a favourable reference to the efforts the CASSL was making 'to induce articled clerks to undergo a systematic and continuous course of study throughout the period of their articles'. Other Societies were devising such schemes. However,

> The articled clerk, ..., who makes use of the facilities offered, has in view the immediate rather than the more distant future; his aim is to pass his examinations within the period of his articles, and I think it will be generally conceded that articled clerks do not, as a rule, extend their studies to subjects outside the scope of the examination papers.
>
> If this is admitted, it follows that the theoretical education offered to articled clerks by the Students' Societies must, as a rule, be confined to the subjects comprised in the Institute examination syllabus.

Cutforth then asked the question

> Is the present examination syllabus the best that can be devised for ensuring that the most efficient and best equipped men are admitted into the profession?

Cutforth admitted to a certain diffidence in dealing with such matters, remembering that

> ... the Council of the Institute of Chartered Accountants has sat for some thirty years without considering it advisable to make

> a single alteration in the form of any Intermediate or Final Examination paper.

Cutforth put before his audience an analysis of the examination papers of the Chartered Accountants of Scotland and the Society of Incorporated Accountants and Auditors. As regards the accountancy and auditing questions set by ICAEW, he concluded that too great a premium was put upon speed and that the length of time available in these examinations should therefore be increased. He referred to the advice of an examination coach as regards preparation for the bookkeeping papers, and the scoring of the greatest number of marks in the limited time available, commenting:

> Now, this may be quite good advice to an examination candidate, but it is the worst possible advice to a student who has a wider object in view than the mere passing of examinations.

Cutforth considered the possibility that ICAEW should introduce a paper on Actuarial Science. He was, however, more positive in a recommendation that Political Economy should be included. Thus

> Many a student can recite the graduated percentages of Estate Duty, but does not know what the Bank Rate means; he can tell you the amounts of the various penalties laid down in the Companies Act, but has hardly heard of the laws of supply and demand; he has the Acts of Bankruptcy at his fingers' ends, but is incapable of writing even a passably good letter or report upon the most simple of matters.

Cutforth referred to report writing as one most desirable skill which the then existing examinations did little or nothing to develop. He noted

> So long as speed is made a <u>sine qua non</u> in the examinations, so long will the standard of report writing remain low. But if ample time were allowed to answer papers on General Commercial Knowledge and on Auditing, I think that the introduction into such papers of questions to test candidates' abilities in report or precis writing would have very beneficial effects.

He summarised his views thus

> <u>Firstly</u>, insufficient time is given in which to answer the accountancy questions.
>
> <u>Secondly</u>, too great a prominence is given in the legal papers to matters of detailed procedure.
>
> <u>Thirdly</u>, no questions are set upon Political Economy or General Commercial Knowledge.

The effect on the students is that:-

(1) They are apt to consider speed of more value than thoroughness, care, and accuracy.

(2) They are compelled to devote too large a proportion of their time to the study of purely legal subjects.

(3) They are encouraged to memorise facts rather than to grasp and understand principles, and are therefore led to neglect general reading for 'cramming'.

A similar general inclination is noticeable in a lecture Cutforth gave in 1913 to the CA Students' Society of Bristol on 'The Organisation of an Accountant's Department' (The Accountant, 10 May, 1913). He chose to outline for his hearers 'the principles governing the organisation of the accountant's department' of a railway company, and it is interesting as an indicator of the degree of specialisation existing among firms of chartered accountants that he should have introduced his remarks as follows:

> I do not suppose that many of you have come into contact with Railway Accounts, nor do I imagine that the majority of you will ever have such an experience. But I hope you will not on this account think that my remarks cannot be of any interest to you. The reason why I am asking you to follow in your mind's eye the control over the transactions of a railway is because I believe that if you grasp the principles underlying the system of control you will be able to apply these principles to other large concerns with which you may come into contact as accountants or auditors.

At the close of his lecture he included the following remarks indicative, first, of his concern that students should seek to acquire a wide grasp of their subjects and give primacy to clarity in thought and expression, and, second, of two separate areas of specialisation (amalgamations and foreign currency translations) in which he was in future years to establish a particular reputation; thus

> A very noticeable feature during the last decade is the growing tendency for large undertakings to become larger still, and for small undertakings to be amalgamated or absorbed. Another noticeable feature is the closer business relationships and community of interests which exist between the various countries of the globe, the consequence of which is that transactions tend to become more complicated, and their effects more obscure.

Cutforth continued:

> And what do these developments teach us as professional accountants? They teach us, I think, that if we are to maintain the reputation which we at present enjoy, if our services to the public are to be no less valuable in the future than they have been in the past, we must move with the times. We

> must equip ourselves to undertake the altered duties and responsibilities which the altered conditions impose upon us. We must try to take a wider grasp of affairs, to cultivate clearness both in thought and expression, to develop our sense of proportion, to look on matters from the broad as well as from the academic standpoint - and all this without becoming one whit less methodical, one whit less accurate, one whit less sound accountants.
>
> We may still find it necessary to examine individual transactions through a microscope, but do not let us forget that it is equally important to take a more distant, and therefore a more comprehensive, view of the transactions as a whole. And in the case of large undertakings, where the scrutiny of every individual transaction is as unnecessary as it is physically impossible, the value of the comprehensive view becomes accentuated.

After the war, changes in the Institute's examinations were made, very much in line with Cutforth's ideas. A new paper, 'General Commercial Knowledge, including the principles and uses of Bookkeeping', was introduced into the ICAEW's Intermediate Examination in November 1921. The following year, an extra half-day was added to the Final Examination, on which candidates were required to take a paper in one of (a) Economics, (b) Banking, Currency and Foreign Exchanges, or (c) Actuarial Science.

In 1913, Cutforth already had a little book <u>Treatment of Fluctuating Currency in Accounts</u> in Gee & Co.'s list at 2/6d. He was to publish a larger book, <u>Foreign Exchange</u>: <u>The Treatment of Fluctuating Currency in the Accounts of English Companies</u> in 1925; and at the Fourth International Congress on Accounting in London in 1933 he presented a paper on 'Exchange Fluctuations in relation to Accounting as regards operating results and asset values' (Proceedings, 67-99). He was lecturing also on 'Report Writing' in the '20s (e.g. <u>The Accountant</u> of 10 January 1925), and had a small book with the same title published by Gee & Co. in 1925: a second edition was printed in 1934.

<u>Amalgamations</u>

Arthur Cutforth had already remarked in 1913 on the tendency of businesses to increase in size, especially through amalgamations or other forms of combination. Movement in these directions was accelerated during and after the war. The subject was to become an outstanding professional interest with him, and Cutforth was to be recognised as a leading authority (in his day, <u>the</u> leading authority) in the field.

He gave a lecture in October 1919 to the CA Students' Society of London with the title: 'Amalgamation Schemes: from an Accountant's point of view' (The Accountant, 3 January 1920, pp.11-24). The object was to identify and consider in some detail the advantages and disadvantages of three principal forms of amalgamation: amalgamation of interests by means of a pooling agreement; amalgamation by acquisition of the whole or a controlling interest in the share capital of one or more companies by a parent or holding company; or a complete amalgamation whereby one company buys the business of another company (that company being then wound up) or where a new company is formed to buy the businesses of two or more existing companies, which are then wound up. Cutforth spoke as a practical accountant with substantial experience in the field. The researcher may guess at an association over the years with Lord Plender's work in the same area, and note that expertise in these and related matters, a broad informed approach, and investigative experience, would have been among the factors leading to Cutforth's appointment to various governmental committees and enquiries in the '20s and '30s. Accountants naturally give the highest attention to confidentiality in clients' affairs: work in the preparation and negotiation of schemes of amalgamation must stress confidentiality in an extreme degree. In later years, Arthur Cutforth's reaction to changing attitudes relative to some aspects of disclosure in company financial reporting may have been influenced by the highly confidential nature of the work he undertook in relation to business mergers.

Cutforth was Accountant Assessor to the Royal Commission on the Coal Industry (the Sankey Commission) in 1925. He was created CBE the following year. In 1926 also he published his major book, Methods of Amalgamation and the valuation of businesses for amalgamation and other purposes (G. Bell & Sons Ltd., London, pp.298). It was the first of its kind. Cutforth's Preface began

> No book on the subject of 'Amalgamations' appears to have been published in this country, although many amalgamations of industrial and other concerns have taken place within recent years ...

Cutforth dealt with circumstances leading to amalgamations, objectives, and objections, and developed the theme under the three heads used in his 1919 lecture, namely complete amalgamations, holding company schemes, and mergers by means of pooling agreements. He followed this with three chapters on valuation of fixed assets, valuation of floating and miscellaneous assets (placing heavy emphasis in both on the use and instruction of professional valuers) and valuation of goodwill, acknowledging in his Preface a debt in this last area to Dicksee and Leake.

Cutforth provided a short additional chapter on 'Valuation of Businesses or undertakings, for purposes of amalgamation, on basis of earning capacity only', though he confined his examples here to cases - a water supply undertaking and a mining property such as a colliery (and elsewhere in the book to a gas undertaking, or a railway) - where there was no ready alternative, and he did not develop the 'earning capacity' method for general application. His chapter on complete amalgamations includes (p.30) what he offers as an 'assertion':

> ... namely that the extent to which the individual assets comprising a business should be valued as a means of arriving at the value of the business as a whole, and the extent to which the earning capacity of the business should be the guide to the value of that busines, depend on the nature and circumstances of the business.

Despite this 'assertion', the weight of Cutforth's argument and presentation was towards business valuation based on the going concern values of individual assets (determined mainly by valuation, and excluding any goodwill element in the individual asset values) plus a value for goodwill ascertained (again despite reservations, but according to the weight of his argument and presentation) by means of the Leake super-profits method. Cutforth paid substantial attention to problems of ascertaining a figure of net profits, and thereafter a figure of super-profits, and capitalisation of the latter 'for purposes of computing goodwill'.

Cutforth's book included an interesting chapter on appropriate capitalisation schemes for a range of companies in various circumstances, and ended with a chapter on valuations of businesses other than for amalgamation purposes. Here, he foresaw the likelihood that a willing seller might not find a willing buyer, and finished tersely (p.229):

> To put it briefly, 'a business is worth what it will fetch'; and what a business will fetch depends on the circumstances surrounding the actual or assumed sale.

Cutforth's Amalgamations made a considerable impact, and amongst other recognitions he was invited to give two public lectures on the subject at the London School of Economics (extracts were printed in The Accountant of 1 January

1927). Lord Plender took the chair on the occasion of the first lecture, and included the following paragraph among his remarks:

> Apart altogether from its peculiar importance at the present time, /the subject of Amalgamations is one which/ embraces, or at least touches, many other subjects of special interest to students of financial and economic problems. It teaches us something of how great enterprises are organised and administered; it gives us an insight into the methods by which businesses are valued; it helps us to appreciate the benefits which large combines, properly regulated, may render to the community, or, alternatively, the harm they may do if their power is misused.

Secrecy versus openness in financial reporting

After the 1928/29 legislation, G. Bell & Son published their second book for Cutforth in 1930 with the title Public Companies and the Investor, which included a Chapter on 'Combines owned and controlled by public companies'. Amongst other things, this referred to holding company groups and outlined the disclosure requirements of the 1929 Companies Act. Cutforth had previously noted that it was unnecessary for the actual names of the subsidiary companies to be disclosed, and included the following comments at the end of his chapter when favourably contrasting a holding company scheme with a complete amalgamation (p.175):

> Under a Holding Company scheme, knowledge of the merging of interests will not be so widespread, as each of the companies continues to operate under its own name; indeed, it is possible by certain special means to confine the knowledge to the Board of Directors of the Holding Company. Usually, however, the financial world is aware of the situation, though the man in the street may not be so.
>
> It is a question for the Directors of companies concerned in a combine to decide as to how far in regard to this matter of disclosure they should take the shareholders into their confidence. It must be remembered that it is, practically speaking, impossible to afford the information to shareholders without giving it also to competitors ...

Cutforth had included a similar reference in Methods of Amalgamation ... (p.76) among 'the special advantages of a Pooling Agreement', thus:

> In the first place, there is the possible advantage of secrecy. The companies owning the businesses in question may be openly engaged in competition and it may be considered inexpedient that the suppliers, customers and the public generally should know that their interests are really identical. The terms of

> the agreement would be negotiated and settled by the Boards of each Company; and although, in the ordinary way, the Directors would consider it necessary to obtain the consent of the shareholders to any action of far-reaching importance, yet under the special circumstances they might well think - and be right in thinking - that, in the best interests of the shareholders themselves, the strictest secrecy was demanded.

The History of the ICAEW and its Founder Bodies refers (p.75) to the Kylsant case of 1931 noting that it 'shook the whole business world and caused great distress and anxiety throughout the profession'. The History continues (p.77):

> The comments of the Council of the Institute upon this important and difficult case were eagerly awaited by members. The learned judge had emphasized that a statement true in every published particular might nevertheless give a false impression as a result of the suppression of material information. In his speech at the Annual General Meeting in 1932, the President, H.L.H. Hill, explained that the Council had decided to issue no directive to members and was not prepared to lay down general principles for guidance arising out of the circumstances of the Royal Mail case. The Council had been advised not to make any official pronouncement on matters which by their very nature were incapable of reduction to exact formulae. Distinguished counsel had been consulted and the President said that, while it was clear that a need existed for raising the standard of disclosure practised in connection with company profit and loss accounts, the Council of the Institute thought that any reform should be effected through the influence of individual members and that there was no need for further legislation.

The History observes that in some quarters, however, there was considerable pressure for further reform of the law and mentions the Association of British Chambers of Commerce and the Society of Incorporated Accountants and Auditors in this regard. The former were active in seeking legislative change, and the Society of Incorporated Accountants and Auditors had set up a special committee to review relevant companies' legislation. Their committee had reported in April 1932 and made a number of recommendations, concluding that the only effective action lay in amending legislation.

The international congress of accountants held in London in 1933 provided opportunities for further discussion, official and private. In 1933 also, Mr. Horace B. Samuel, a barrister and financial consultant, published his Shareholders' Money which made a comprehensive and critical attack on the limited disclosures of the 1929 companies' legislation. Samuel argued strongly for a new statute and included a draft bill in his book. In the USA also, discussions were in process, leading to the securities and exchange legislation of 1933/34.

Arthur Cutforth was Vice President in 1932/33 and 1933/34, on the first occasion in support of Mr. Clare Smith, President for that year, and on the second in support of Mr. H.L.H. Hill who had been President in 1931/32 and was chosen again for that office in 1933/34. The Accountant observed (17 June 1933, p.802) that the fact that Mr. Hill had been chosen as President for the year in which the International Congress was being held was a tribute to the success with which he carried out his duties in 1931/32. The Accountant added that he would have a most able Vice President in Mr. Cutforth.

At the 1933 Annual Meeting, Mr. Clare Smith in his Presidential Address had noted that the question of amending the 1929 Companies Act had received a good deal of attention in the press and in public speeches during the past twelve months. He continued:

> The questions raised are not easy of solution, but if and when the Parliamentary machine can find time again to consider the amendment of the Companies Acts, /the/ question of subsidiary companies will probably be one of the most important subjects to be debated. I expect, however, that we shall have, for the present, to content ourselves by endeavouring, under the existing law to make the accounts of limited companies somewhat more informative, and I think I may say that signs are not wanting that directors are more ready to confer with their auditors and listen to their views than was the case some years ago.

This was in line with Mr. H.L.H. Hill's statement of a year earlier. Lord Plender in his April 1932 Presidential Address to the CASSL had taken the same line.

The History of the ICAEW noted (p.76) that after Kylsant, the 'question of secret reserves came up for discussion whenever accountants met together'. Lord Plender commented in April 1932:

> The average investor is not, I think, averse to directors adopting a prudent and cautious policy for strengthening the financial position of a company by reasonable inner provisions for contingencies which overtake most companies at some period of their existence ... I cannot say that compulsory disclosure on a balance sheet of the amounts of all such inner provisions or reserves would be desirable in every case, and so long as they are made honestly and prudently and with the intent that the company's best interests shall be served, there are many advantages and often considerable justification for their existence.

This was an echo of the ICAEW's evidence to the Greene Committee in 1925. Lord Plender went on:

> Accounts should not hide the truth - they should reveal it. And the test ... when a balance sheet is being reported upon by

> an auditor is, does it convey to the shareholders such information as will enable them to ascertain fairly the position of the company's business as a going concern, bearing in mind, of course, the limitation to which a balance sheet, by its nature, is subject? If not, he should qualify his report to the shareholders.

Arthur Cutforth, as President in 1934/35 and 1935/36, followed the same line. In a Presidential Address at the 1934 Autumnal Meeting, he drew a connection between anxieties for legislative change and the disturbances created in the minds of investors by the financial crises of 1929-32 and the subsequent depression. Cutforth argued for the various suggestions made to be further examined calmly and dispassionately so as to consider 'how far they are practicable and whether, if practicable, they are calculated to be beneficial'. Earlier that year, whilst still Vice President, he had given a lecture to the Chartered Institute of Secretaries to the same general effect. In his final Presidential Address at the Annual Meeting in 1936 he noted that a year ago he had mentioned that the Government thought it preferable to defer consideration of revision of the Companies Act until more experience had been accumulated, and added that no change in the situation has since occurred. He said:

> There is a general consensus of opinion that in certain respects the Act requires amendment; but in the judgement of many it is preferable that the whole Act should be carefully reviewed with the object of ascertaining what modifications and additions are needed rather than that certain matters which obviously call for reconsideration should be made the subject of immediate legislation.

In the meantime Boards of Directors of reporting companies, led by the Dunlop Rubber Co. amongst others, had been taking substantial steps in the direction of greater openness and disclosure in financial reporting, as the Council had hoped they would when it took its unpopular decision four years previously. Mr. Roger N. Carter, who followed Cutforth as President in 1936/37 maintained the views of his predecessors in his Presidential Address at the 1937 Annual Meeting when he noted that:

> ... in the meantime the profession itself is directing attention to more information being afforded both in the balance sheet and in the profit and loss account. It is probable that this can be better achieved in that way than by legislation.

The leading members of the Council of the ICAEW through those years carried a great responsibility in holding to their chosen line of action in the face of widespread criticism. How far they were right to do so must remain a matter of judgement.

Cutforth's contribution

It is beyond question that Arthur Cutforth made a substantial contribution as a leading practitioner and a loyal member of and spokesman for the Council of the ICAEW. Through his books and other writings (and it is for these especially that he is distinguished here) he made an important contribution to accounting ideas and to the development of the profession, most notably of all in the area of amalgamations. His review, in 1912, of examination requirements for the ICAEW bore fruit after the War and brought some general consideration of economic aspects into the accountancy curriculum. Perhaps we should not complain that by the 1930s Cutforth's innovative drive seemed to have spent its force.

CHAPTER 7

FREDERIC RUDOLPH MACKLEY de PAULA, CBE, FCA
1882-1954

Frederic de Paula brought charm and an exceptional capacity to a remarkably wide span of activities ranging from the centre to the circumference of the accountancy profession and beyond it. In all of these he achieved distinction: as student, teacher, practitioner, and author; as war-time administrator in two world wars; as university lecturer and professor, albeit part-time; as accountant and financial manager in industry; as standard-bearer in the movement for fuller disclosure and greater comprehensibility in financial reporting; as the first non-practising member of the Council of the Institute of Chartered Accountants in England and Wales (ICAEW); as a main progenitor of the ICAEW's important Recommendations on Accounting Principles which began to appear under his Vice-Chairmanship and Chairmanship of the ICAEW's Taxation and Financial Relations Committee early in the 1940s (and which brought to fruition a sufficient revolution in professional attitudes to transform within a few years both accounting practice and legislation on financial reporting); as successful industrialist and director of important companies; and as educationist. It was a minor personal tragedy that, at the end of his career, his fresh mind and forward thinking on education for the accountancy profession isolated him from some old friends and respected colleagues. His fault was that he thought and spoke in advance of his time. Had Frederic de Paula lived another dozen years, he would have seen the kind of educational reforms he advocated well on the way to acceptance as the new orthodoxy. de Paula's ideas were influential well beyond Britain, and brought him a circle of friends around the world.

Family

Frederic Rudolph Mackley de Paula was born on 23 July 1882 at Avenue House, Tenterden Grove, Hendon. Frederic's grandmother had come over from Germany to settle in Britain, and her son, Friedrich Moritz Alphonse Felix de Paula (Frederic's father) became a solicitor and partner in a City solicitors' practice (Carey, Warburton and de Paula) at 3 West Street, Finsbury Circus, EC from about 1876. The firm moved to 16 Finsbury Circus some twenty years later. Friedrich Moritz de Paula died in Greece in October 1902, leaving a widow

(Ellen Harriet de Paula, nee Mackley), another son besides Frederic (Waldemar Max de Paula, who was to become a respected City stockbroker) and three daughters.

In 1912, Frederic de Paula married Agnes Smithson Clark in Street, Somerset. She was the daughter of Francis Joseph Clark, boot and shoe manufacturer of that town. The Clarks were a well-known Quaker family, and the marriage was solemnized at the Friends' Meeting House in Street according to the usages of the Religious Society of Friends. The Quaker influence was to be a lasting one. Without doubt it supported Frederic's own strong independence of mind, and it revealed itself in small matters also: at his death, Frederic's will included the express wish 'that no mourning shall be worn by anyone'. There were two sons of Frederic's marriage to Agnes Clark, Hugh Francis Mackley de Paula, and Frederic Clive de Paula.

After her husband's death, Frederic's mother lived for a time in North Finchley, and later at 'Netherdale', Nether Street, Church End, Finchley. That address was Frederic's home at the time of his marriage. Frederic and Agnes were to live for many years in Radlett, Hertfordshire, where they are remembered at the Porters Park Golf Club (they became Captain and Lady Captain respectively); and there was a London house at 49 Eaton Terrace, SW1 from about 1921, and later flats in Kensington and Knightsbridge. Frederic was aged 72 when he died in December 1954. His wife was seven years his junior. She survived him and, indeed, happily is still living at the time these notes are being written.

Early years in the profession

Frederic de Paula was articled in 1901 to C.F. Cape (Charles F. Cape & Co.) of 12 Coleman Street, EC. In later years, Frederic was heard to allege that he had to learn quickly because of Cape's taste for hunting in the winter, when he left his clerks to do the work of the practice. Frederic took his Intermediate examination in December 1903, and his Final in December 1905, being placed 5th in order of merit in the first (out of 162 candidates) and seventh in order of merit in the second (out of 195 candidates). At each of these examinations, the first place in order of merit was taken by Gilbert Garnsey, who had been articled in Walsall to N.G. Harries, of Harries and Higgison, chartered accountants, who practised in Walsall with offices also in Birmingham and Wolverhampton. Garnsey was a few months younger than de Paula. He was to have a career of exceptional brilliance, with a partnership in Price Waterhouse

Mr. F. R. M. de PAULA, O.B.E., F.C.A.

From *The Accountant*, 26 June 1926

& Co. from 1913, a knighthood in 1918, and a reputation thoroughly established by the early 1920s as favouring increased disclosure in the published accounts of companies, especially holding companies. He died in 1932 at the early age of 49.

After qualifying, de Paula remained for a time as clerk with C.F. Cape & Co. He went into practice on his own account in 1909, beginning modestly at 12 Coleman Street. He had already developed an interest in teaching, and in October 1908 was providing the Auditing lectures for the Finals students of the C.A. Students' Society of London. Lawrence Dicksee (lately resigned from his part-time Chair at Birmingham, and already into his seventh academic year as part-time Lecturer at LSE) was still, in 1908/09, giving the Bookkeeping and Accounts lectures for the CASSL Finalists. de Paula was to take on Dicksee's Bookkeeping and Accounts lectures, in addition to his own Auditing course, in October 1910.

de Paula's work as a practitioner began to show promise, and he was joined in practice in 1910 by Edgar John Turner. They worked together as de Paula, Turner & Co. at 58 Leadenhall Street, EC, until 1913, when they were in turn joined by John Strickland Lake and the firm's name was extended to de Paula, Turner, Lake & Co., then of 56a Leadenhall Street. The practice still continues under the same name in the City, though Frederic de Paula resigned his partnership in 1929 (see below).

de Paula's teaching work in auditing left him increasingly dissatisfied with the texts available, then mainly Pixley's, Dicksee's, and Cutforth's books. He decided to write his own, and did so in the Spring and Summer of 1914. Pitmans published the first edition of Principles of Auditing later that year. Despite the upheaval of the war, the book was successful: a second edition appeared in 1917 and a third in 1920. Frederic de Paula undertook his last major revision of the text for the eleventh edition in 1951, three years before he died.

Principles of Auditing, like Cutforth's Audits, was written primarily for students. de Paula said as much in his Preface to the first edition, adding that his object had been to produce a book of convenient size at a reasonable price. To shorten the book, de Paula, like Cutforth, eliminated reprinted sections of Acts of Parliament (apart from sections of the Companies Act); but unlike Cutforth, he also omitted certain matters, such as the particular problems arising in audits or investigations for different classes of undertakings and specialised companies, to which both Cutforth and Dicksee made extensive, though rather superficial, reference. de Paula's aim was to provide a deeper foundation and to

> cover the whole of the ground-work with which every student of auditing must be familiar, ... to explain the principles and reasons underlying each subject dealt with ... /and/ adequately to discuss the important root-principles that apply to every audit.

A hundred examination questions set out 'in order with the text of the book' were included in an Appendix.

de Paula had put much preliminary thought into two lectures on auditing (stressing the need to supplement 'routine checking' with intelligent inquiry and research) which he had delivered to a number of CA Students' Societies in 1911 and 1912, beginning with the CASS of Hull (reproduced in The Accountant of 15 June 1912 and 22 March 1913). He had presented an earlier, more specialised, lecture in 1909 on 'The audit and investigation of the accounts of Executors and Trustees' (The Accountant, 9 April 1910).

Robert H. Montgomery, who had edited the first and second authorized American editions of Dicksee's Auditing, in 1905 and 1909, had published his own Auditing Theory and Practice in 1912 on the grounds that Dicksee's book no longer met the needs of the profession in the USA where 'much more work /was being done/ in audits than was called for' in 'Dicksee'. In Britain, by 1915, when Dicksee's tenth edition was published, The Accountant's reviewer (amongst many favourable observations) was noting that

> The book has now passed through so many editions that parts of it have assumed a slightly patchwork appearance, and we would suggest that those portions dealing with matters which have been subject to changing conditions should be completely re-written before the book again goes through the press ... (The Accountant, 10 July 1915, p.54)

When de Paula's Principles appeared, Dicksee's book was already more than twenty years old. de Paula had said in his 1913 Student Society lecture

> ... nowadays far more is expected from an auditor and a far greater knowledge is required than was the case in years gone by ...

de Paula's views were justified by the success of his book.

The First World War: experience of large-scale administration

When William Cash gave his Presidential Address at the ICAEW's Autumnal Meeting in London in 1921, he noted that the previous Autumnal Meeting had been that of 1913. Speaking of the war, he said (inter alia)

> ... perhaps the most important work undertaken by members of our body was in connection with the new Government Departments, organised to meet war exigencies, and at the War Office and the Admiralty, at the Ministry of Munitions, and in the Government Trading Departments in food, timber, sugar, etc., by advice, in organisation in financial control, in regulation of contracts, there were found most of the leaders of the profession, and a very large number of the younger members also, whose training and capabilities were invaluable in setting in motion and carrying on the enormous undertakings that were created for the necessities of the war.

Frederic de Paula was amongst the younger practitioners who left their firms for such work. He was first employed at the Ministry of Munitions in the Gun Ammunition Filling Department under Sir Eric Geddes. de Paula was concerned with organising the statistical section of the Department, first under George Beharrell, and later, when Beharrell went to France, as Director of that section in his stead. At the beginning of 1917, de Paula was commissioned and joined the staff in France of Sir Eric Geddes, at that time Director-General of Transportation at General Headquarters. de Paula became an Assistant Director-General of Transportation with the rank of Lieut. Colonel. He was gazetted OBE (military division) and twice mentioned in despatches. de Paula was demobilised in September 1919, whereafter he returned to his practice.

His war-time experience of large-scale organisation and administration made a deep impression on him. It was to work again with Sir Eric Geddes and Sir George Beharrell that de Paula went in 1929 to the Dunlop Rubber Company as Chief Accountant, and later as Financial Controller.

The London School of Economics and Political Science

Reference has been made above to Lawrence Dicksee's appointment in 1919 to the then newly created Sir Ernest Cassel Chair of Accountancy and Business Methods in the University of London, tenable at LSE. The 1919 appointment to an established Chair was a part-time one, and Dicksee had, at that date, already held a personal appointment as Professor (part-time) at LSE for five years. The Sir Ernest Cassel foundations in 1919 included Chairs in Banking and

Currency, and International Relations, as well as in Accountancy, which along with three Readerships and three Lectureships, were to assist the University to establish its new degree in Commerce at LSE.

By the beginning of the 1920/21 academic year provision had been made for the full Commerce curriculum to be offered to students, and Frederic de Paula had joined Dicksee at LSE as Lecturer (part-time) with him in the courses on Accounting and Business Methods. Dicksee himself gave the courses in 'Business Organisation' and 'Cost Accounts and Efficiency Methods' as they were called. Reference has been made earlier to Dicksee's 'Army Class' at LSE from 1906/7 onwards. In the early 1920s, many of the students taught by Dicksee and de Paula at LSE were demobilised officers. These sustained the interests of both men in general problems of large-scale administration and in the particular problems facing returning servicemen. In 1924 the institution of a Readership in Accounting and Business Organisation was announced and de Paula was appointed to the post, again on a part-time basis.

When Dicksee retired in 1926, Frederic de Paula followed him as Professor of Accountancy and Business Methods, holding that appointment (part-time) until December 1929, when he resigned his Chair, and his position as senior partner in de Paula, Turner, Lake & Co., to join Dunlops.

Interests and ideas in the 1920s

In addition to his work at LSE, Frederic de Paula continued in the 1920s to give formal lectures to outside groups such as 'The Detection of Fraud in Accounts' to various CA Students' Societies in 1920 and 1921, and 'The Interpretation of Accounts' to the Institute of Book-keepers in March 1926 (republished, with other similar material, in de Paula's Developments in Accounting 1948). Broadly, these followed his general approach in Principles of Auditing: the former stressed that to discover fraud '... an auditor must go behind the actual books of account, and examine original records and make intelligent inquiries ...'; the latter ended with a reference to changing attitudes to disclosure in published accounts thus,

> ... in my opinion there is room for improvement in the form in which published Balance Sheets are presented, and evolution upon these lines would greatly assist in the interpretation of the accounts of commercial concerns. The policy of secrecy has been overstressed ...

We may presume that de Paula had been present in October 1925 at a London Members' lunch chaired by Sir Gilbert Garnsey, at which Sir Josiah Stamp had given (in an address reproduced in The Accountant of 31 October 1925) what he called an 'outsider's reflections' on 'Accountants' Problems of Today', in particular on information presented in balance sheets. Sir Josiah was known to be strongly antagonistic to secret reserves, and Garnsey in 1925 had lately come under criticism from within the profession for his championship of consolidated balance sheets and consolidated profit and loss accounts for holding company groups.

Speaking in 1921 to the Annual Conference of the Incorporated Accountants in Liverpool, Sir Josiah Stamp had said, *inter alia*,

> ... deliberate upon the sorry figure that is cut ... by ... a 'safe' or 'sound' balance sheet, which lies in almost every line and yet is approved ... because it overstates no assets and understates no liabilities ... prudence ... is just as possible without departing from what a balance sheet ought to be - a faithful record of the employment of the total capital invested in the business ...

That there were important and widely held views to the contrary may be judged from the Memorandum of Evidence submitted by the Council of the ICAEW in July 1925 to the Greene Committee on Company Law Amendment. This took a strong line against further disclosure by prescription. Thus:

> The conditions under which companies carry on their business are so numerous, the nature of the business so varied and the places at which the businesses are carried on so spread over the world that to attempt to prescribe either a statutory form of balance sheet or what a balance sheet must disclose or that there should be in addition a profit and loss account is considered likely to do more harm than good.
>
> Shareholders have the remedy to a large extent in their own hands. They can and do ask questions at the annual meetings. The business done by limited companies is, on the whole, transacted by directors and managers who are honest, and if in some cases they disclose in the published accounts less than some people desire the absence of detail is in most cases wise and is generally supported by the shareholders.

On 'secret reserves' the Memorandum of Evidence said, *inter alia*:

> Secret Reserves or Inner Reserves are in certain cases desirable and in many cases essential ...
>
> If businesses carried on by joint stock companies are to be as successful in the future as in the past, too much disclosure should not be insisted on and the greatest possible freedom should be allowed to those responsible.

> It is always open to the auditors to report to the shareholders any exceptional reserves which are made or written back or other special matters dealt with in the accounts if the directors do not disclose them on the face of the accounts or in their report to the shareholders.

The ICAEW Memorandum of Evidence took a similar line as regards the accounts of holding companies and their subsidiaries, thus:

> It is considered undesirable to prescribe by legislation any rule for dealing in the accounts of Holding Companies with their subsidiaries. The circumstances under which such holdings arise are so varied and the places where such businesses are carried on are in some cases so spread over the world that to lay down any hard and fast rule would do more harm than good.
>
> In the opinion of the Council the form of the balance sheet should as at present be left to the directors and shareholders. To prepare a consolidated balance sheet would not show the true position of the company, so long as the subsidiaries are separate entities. If the accounts of subsidiary companies had by legislation to be made up to the same date as the parent company and incorporated in that company's published accounts, by the time the details were received by the parent company for incorporation, the accounts of the parent company would in some cases be ancient history.
>
> The question of whether or not what has been described as the legal balance sheet should be supplemented by other balance sheets is a matter entirely for the directors and shareholders.

At the October 1925 lunch, Sir Josiah directed his main attention to the disadvantages of secret reserves, though he did not, on that occasion, condemn them in such strong terms as in 1921. He also declared himself firmly in favour of consolidated accounts for holding company groups, thus:

> The consolidated balance sheet is familiar enough in America, but is only beginning to be known in this country. It can be developed with appropriate public education to understand it, and it is at any rate better than giving a sheaf of subsidiary accounts without nexus which bewilder the average shareholder ...
>
> It seems to me that there can be nothing to be said against the publication of consolidated balance sheets in conjunction with the legal balance sheet, and everything to be said for it. Only in time will its full significance be appreciated. I am not pleading for wholesale legal action. It will grow by the establishment of the best as a practice, and the best is not necessarily what is oldest until it is shaken up by some abuse in a law court ...

Six years afterwards in 1931, the Kylsant case was to remind many of these words.

Sir Josiah Stamp's remarks provoked a leading article in The Accountant (31 October 1925) and a little flurry of correspondence. Three weeks later, The Accountant presented two contributed comments on Sir Josiah's address, one by Mr. Jonas Hambley (who represented, broadly, what might be termed 'traditional' reactions) and the other - a rather longer one, which appeared in short parts over three weeks - by Frederic de Paula, who offered what we might call a more notably 'progressive' response. It is worth recalling a few sentences from de Paula's comments, viz.:

> The arguments in favour of the secret reserve, the condensed balance sheet, and the legal balance sheet of the holding company, are well-known to all accountants, but are these arguments really sound? If all reserves were shown openly in the balance sheet and reverses were charged thereto, would the public credit of the concern be shaken? If a full balance sheet were published what use could competitors ... make of the information revealed?
>
> My own view is that the arguments in favour of secrecy are exaggerated, and that from the point of view of the community the policy is a mistaken one, as it is creating a feeling of distrust. However, it is only by the weight of public opinion that this policy will be abandoned, but in my opinion more open methods will have to be adopted in the future and Sir Josiah Stamp is right in asking accountants to face these problems now, with a view to using their influence in the direction of changes of method which are inevitable.
> (The Accountant, 21 November 1925, p.802)

Later in his comments, de Paula offered an observation which has a distinctly modern ring:

> To my mind the peculiarity of the legal position /of the auditor of a company/ is that the value of the auditor's advice and opinions is available to the management, whom he does not represent, but is not fully available to the shareholders, whose agent he is.
> (The Accountant, 5 December 1925, p.888)

The accountant in commerce and industry

Frederic de Paula's most important public lecture in the 1920s was delivered at LSE on 14 October 1926 shortly after his appointment to the Sir Ernest Cassel Chair of Accountancy and Business Methods vacated by Lawrence Dicksee upon his retirement in July 1926. Dicksee had been granted the title of Emeritus Professor and it was he who acted as chairman at de Paula's lecture, 'The Place of Accountancy in Commerce'. (Developments in Accounting, pp.135-147.)

de Paula was concerned to stress that the importance of Accounts Departments in commerce and industry had long been growing, but that, in his view, there were great possibilities for further development, in which he saw the professional accountant as being in a position to play an important part. However, de Paula expressed the opinion that substantial further progress would not be possible until the commercial world was convinced as to 'the great possibilities of accountancy and the great help which it can give to the management of every business concern'.

de Paula looked to re-organisation upon the lines of:

> raising the whole status of the accounts department, which should rank equally with the principal executive departments. The chief accountant should not be merely the head book-keeper but he should be the chief financial officer of the concern, being responsible to the general manager for the whole of the finances of the business and its financial control ... The chief accountant should ... have a wide knowledge of business organisation, business generally and finance, and further, it would be necessary for him to have a highly trained staff under him.
>
> The chief accountant ... should represent finance, it being his duty to report upon the financial aspects of every proposition under consideration.

de Paula listed the principal functions of the accounts department of a manufacturing concern under eleven heads, as under:

> 1. The control of the whole of the book-keeping records, which should be organised upon modern time-saving methods.
>
> 2. The control of the stores and costing system.
>
> 3. The control of a statistical system the objects of which are to record and focus all information of use to the management.
>
> 4. The preparation of weekly and monthly statistical summaries, including monthly Revenue Accounts and Balance Sheets.
>
> 5. The chief accountant should be responsible for the preparation of forecasts of the future requirements - for example: materials, labour, equipment, and capital.
>
> 6. The accounts department should supply the various executive departments with the accounting and statistical information required by them.
>
> 7. The preparation of the annual Manufacturing and Profit and Loss Accounts and Balance Sheet of the concern and reporting thereon to the management.
>
> 8. The settlement with the Revenue of the taxation liabilities of the concern.

> 9. The control of the financial administration of the business and the reporting upon the financial aspects of every proposal under consideration by the management.
>
> 10. The chief accountant should act as financial adviser to the managing director and should report to him the important factors revealed by the accounting and statistical records.
>
> 11. The accounts department should be constantly engaged upon research work and should report upon the present position, future prospects and suggestions as to improvements in the organisation with a view to the economical and efficient conduct of the business.

de Paula developed each of these heads in his lecture, concluding

> I do not wish to give the impression that I am suggesting that the accounts department is the most important of all and that it should be responsible for the practical management of the concern. The accounts department should be the servant of management and its purpose should be to watch and advise upon the financial aspect of affairs, and in this way to assist the management in the control and administration of the concern.

When, three years later, de Paula moved to Dunlops, it was to fulfil just such a role. At his lecture he was speaking primarily to future Commerce graduates, the bulk of whom could be expected to enter employment in industry and commerce. He set an exciting prospect before them.

de Paula presented another lecture with a similar title ('Accounts as an aid to Management') in 1927 to the Office Machinery Users' Association. It is of interest because it stressed the need of management to look ahead, and it was de Paula's argument that the accountant in industry or commerce must do the same. Accordingly, his lecture developed the practical advantages to be obtained through a system of budgetary control.

<u>Education for the accountancy profession</u>

A couple of months after his October 1926 lecture at LSE, de Paula responded to a short series of letters in <u>The Accountant</u> dealing more or less directly with education for the accountancy profession. His name had been among several mentioned in the correspondence (including those of Sir William Plender and Sir Josiah Stamp) as possibly suitable to consider a scheme in which accountancy might be given a place among the honours degrees of universities and thereby form a part (as did the LL.B for lawyers) of the accountants' professional education and training. de Paula's letter (dated 22 December 1926) was brief; he referred to the suggestions of the correspondent concerned saying:

> ... in my opinion the present system of education is far from satisfactory.
>
> The practical work of the average articled clerk is mainly devoted to routine checking, which is of little educational value, and the theoretical studies of the great proportion of students are conducted by the professional 'crammers'. No doubt the results are satisfactory from an examination point of view, but from the point of view of the education of the future members of a great profession the present position, in my opinion, is capable of considerable improvement.
>
> I do not think that any change can be effected until the Councils of the Institute and the Society take a direct interest and concern in the methods of education of their future members.
>
> Considerable progress in the study of accountancy has been made in recent years by the modern universities, and I would suggest that the accountancy profession should take an active interest in this work, as, for example, the legal profession does in the faculty of law.
>
> Those who appreciate the great possibilities for the future development of accountancy, realize that there is a real need in this, as in other branches of human effort, for sustained academic study and research. The commercial world has realized the value and possibilities of this work and the developments to date have been initiated and financed to a considerable extent by such men as the late Sir Ernest Cassel; but so far as I am aware, the Institute and the Society have not directly concerned themselves with the academic study of accountancy or research work, and apart from the setting of examinations and financial support given to Students' societies, they have not concerned themselves directly with the educational methods in force within the profession itself.

Frederic de Paula's letter appeared in The Accountant of 1 January 1927. No further correspondence followed upon it. Mr. Ernest Evan Spicer gave a lecture on 'The Articled Clerk in relation to Education' to CA Students' Societies in Manchester, Birmingham and Cardiff in December 1926 and January 1927, and this was published in The Accountant of 26 March 1927. It proposed wide-ranging (and drastic) reforms: a number of letters followed the lecture, but in 1927 the education issue did not prosper.

The Dunlop Rubber Company Ltd.

Sir Eric Geddes had become a director of the Dunlop Rubber Company in 1922, and its Chairman in 1924. Sir George Beharrell, knighted in 1919, had been appointed Managing Director of Dunlops in 1923. In the later 1920s, Geddes, Beharrell and the Dunlop board were interested in de Paula and in his ideas on the contribution which an accountant could make to the management of a large industrial undertaking such as theirs, which was suffering from financial problems. Frederic de Paula resigned from his practice and from his Chair at LSE, and joined the Dunlop Company on 1 January 1930, in the first instance as Chief Accountant, and shortly afterwards with the title of Controller of Finance. The appointment gave him a splendid opportunity to put his ideas into practice. He grasped it with both hands and his efforts proved immensely successful.

In his Preface to Developments in Accounting, Frederic de Paula refers to his having 'persuaded the board of a public company, of which /he/ was the auditor, to present its accounts in accordance with /his/ ideas' for improved disclosure and comprehensibility. This was Temoh Tin Dredging Ltd., and de Paula records (though he does not name the Company) that the accounts 'were reviewed favourably in The Accountant, The Economist, The Times, and The Financial Times'. The Accountant printed out the Temoh Tin balance sheet at 30 June 1929 and the year's profit and loss account, and these are shown below. They may be left to speak for themselves. Amongst other things, the provision for the proposed net dividend will be noted. This represented another innovation much canvassed by de Paula which was eventually to be universally adopted. de Paula persuaded the Dunlop board to present their 1929 accounts in the general form worked out for Temoh Tin. When the 1931 accounts for Dunlops appeared they again attracted favourable comment at least in part because they included comparative figures for 1930.

In 1931, the Kylsant case startled the City and the business world. It was widely reported in newspapers and periodicals. Full-length books on the subject included C. Brooks (ed.) The Royal Mail Case, and H.B. Samuel, Shareholders' Money, both of which appeared in 1933.

The case turned on the use of secret reserves to bolster the reported profits of the Royal Mail Steam Packet Company (RMSP), of which Lord Kylsant was Chairman. The auditor was Mr. H.J. Morland, a senior partner in Price Waterhouse & Co. They were charged with publishing annual accounts of the Company for 1926 and 1927 which they '... knew to be false in a material particular ... with intent to deceive ...' Both were acquitted, though Lord Kylsant was found guilty and imprisoned on another charge concerning a prospectus, with which Mr. Morland was not associated.

As regards the RMSP accounts, the reference to profits for 1926, which was alleged to be misleading, ran:

TEMOH TIN DREDGING LTD.

BALANCE SHEET AS AT 30TH JUNE 1929

(For the purposes of these Accounts the rate of Exchange has been taken at 2s. 4d. to the Dollar)

	£ s d	£ s d
Capital -		
Authorised:		
150,000 Shares of £1 each	150,000 0 0	
Issued:		
140,000 Shares of £1 each, fully paid	140,000 0 0	
Profit and Loss Account -		
Balance as per Account, after deducting proposed dividend	2,215 16 11	142,215 16 11
Current Liabilities -		
Creditors:		
London	603 7 9	
Eastern	2,219 3 2	
W. Simon & Co. Ltd.	4,450 11 4	
Proposed Dividend of 9d. per Share, less Income Tax	4,200 0 0	11,473 2 3
		£153,688 19 2

	£ s d	£ s d
Fixed Assets -		
Property Account, Mining Leases, &c. (at cost)		62,000 0 0
Dredge:		
Balance as at 1st July 1928 (at cost)	55,001 18 2	
Add Expenditure during the year	5,893 18 4	
	60,895 16 6	
Less Depreciation	1,903 0 0	58,992 16 6
Buildings, Coolie Lines and Bungalows (at cost)	3,187 14 3	
Plant and Machinery (at cost)	335 8 4	
Furniture and Fittings (at cost)	150 14 8	
Loose Tools (at cost)	259 4 3	
Pipe Line and Water Supply Plant (at cost)	4,568 8 3	
Roads and Bridges (at cost)	651 5 0	
	9,152 14 9	
Less Depreciation	312 0 0	8,840 14 9
		129,833 11 3
Miscellaneous Expenditure and Debit Balances -		
Dredge Paddock Excavation as at 1st July 1928 (at cost)	1,628 11 3	
Sundry Expenditure in London and the East, as at 1st July 1928 (at cost)	2,127 18 9	
Preliminary Expenses as at 1st July 1928 (at cost)	2,388 1 11	6,144 11 11
Current Assets -		
Payments in advance	282 13 5	
Stores on hand, as certified by Mine Manager, and Stores in transit	3,123 17 10	
Stock of Tin Ore - at prices since realised	6,827 11 9	
Stock of Rubber on hand - at prices since realised	269 19 4	
Sundry Debtors	36 8 6	
Advances to Contractors in the East	119 10	
Deposit - Federated Malay States Rail	58 6 8	
Bank Balances on Deposit and Current Accounts and Cash in Hand - London and the East	6,992 16 8	17,710 16 0
		£153,688 19 2

TEMOH TIN DREDGING LTD.

PROFIT AND LOSS ACCOUNT FOR THE YEAR ENDED 30TH JUNE 1929

Dr.	£	s	d	£	s	d
To Expenses in the East -						
Superintendence	297	18	4			
Wages and Salaries	4,400	18	7			
Working and Maintenance	4,361	7	7			
Tin Ore Dressing	860	18	11			
Office Expenses, Audit and Sundries	1,112	17	6			
Insurances	318	5	8			
Prospecting	123	14	10	11,476	1	5
" Agency Fee				350	0	0
" Expenses in London -						
Secretarial Fee and Rent, Printing and Stationery, Postages, Cables, Audit Fee and Sundries	541	7	6			
Directors' Fees	500	0	0	1,041	7	6
" Income Tax				293	5	2
" Loss on Exchange				72	13	3
" Depreciation of Dredge, Buildings, Coolie Lines, Plant and Machinery, Furniture and Fittings, &c.				2,215	0	0
				15,448	7	4
" Net Profit for the year carried down				6,415	16	11
				£21,864	4	3

Cr.	£	s	d	£	s	d
By Sales of Tin Ore	13,628	8	9			
" Stock of Tin Ore - at prices since realised	6,827	11	9	20,456	0	6
" Sales of Rubber - less Expenses	920	14	9			
" Stock of Rubber - at prices since realised	269	19	4	1,190	14	1
" Interest on Deposit				217	9	8
				£21,864	4	3

	£	s	d	£	s	d
To Proposed Dividend of 9d. per Share for the year 1928-29	5,250	0	0			
Less Income Tax	1,050	0	0	4,200	0	0
" Balance carried forward				2,215	16	11
				£ 6,415	16	11

	£	s	d
By Net Profit for the year brought down	6,415	16	11
	£ 6,415	16	11

> Balance for the year, including dividends on shares in allied and associated companies, adjustment of taxation reserves, less depreciation on the fleet, etc. ... £439,212: 12: 1.

The words '... including ... adjustment of taxation reserves' had been written in by Mr. Morland on his own initiative when the accounts were in draft. In 1926, the Company had in fact been running at a loss, and the 'profit' was arrived at after crediting £750,000 out of the tax reserves. The issue was whether Mr. Morland had acted in accordance with accepted practice, and expert evidence (which was not challenged) was successfully submitted to show that he had.

Reference has already been made (p.93 above) to the response of the Council of the ICAEW to the Kylsant case. It made a deep impression on de Paula. His Preface to the sixth edition of Principles of Auditing (which appeared in 1933) is worth quoting in full:

> Since the fifth edition of this book was published, the accountancy profession has been shocked by the Royal Mail Steam Packet case. There is no single event in my memory that has made so profound an impression upon the accountancy world, and that case, in my opinion, is destined to influence accountancy practice in a marked degree.
>
> For these reasons I have dealt with this case at some length in this edition, and I have quoted considerable portions of the judge's summing up, as in my view every accountant should study this case most closely.
>
> The questions involved are of great importance, and this case brings to light vividly the vexed question of the creation and utilisation of secret reserves. In the previous edition, upon this subject, I wrote: 'The attitude of auditors as regards secret reserves is being challenged; the whole subject therefore is one which merits serious consideration and upon which some form of uniform practice should be adopted by the profession.'
>
> When I wrote those words I had little idea that that challenge would come so swiftly and in such a serious form.
>
> Upon this subject, collectively, the profession has not made up its mind, nor has it upon many others, e.g. the form in which the accounts of holding companies should be presented and the basis upon which they should be prepared; how the profits and losses of subsidiary and sub-subsidiary companies should be dealt with in the accounts of the holding company; what information should be disclosed in the published Profit and Loss Accounts of companies; the basis of calculation of depreciation of Fixed Assets; the basis of valuation of Stock in Trade and how forward contracts should be dealt with in accounts.
>
> The individual practitioner and the executives of companies responsible for the framing of their accounts naturally turn to the accountancy profession for guidance upon these important points, but though there are many individual opinions - my own are given in this book - there are no accepted and established principles governing these several matters.

> It does seem to me to be of urgent importance that the profession should make up its mind upon these questions. That it has not done so may be due to the fact that the profession has grown so rapidly and, individually, we have been so busily engaged upon our day-to-day tasks that the profession has not yet had time to pause, think these matters out, and collectively to make up its mind as to the correct principles that should govern these questions.

de Paula was to continue to canvass his ideas about the development of a professional view on important and controversial aspects of accounting practice, and a move towards uniformity. The Preface to the sixth edition was dated February 1933: the fifth edition, to which it referred, had been brought out after the 1928-29 companies legislation, in respect of which it incorporated necessary revisions. It is a tribute to de Paula's work, and to the interest shown in his writing, that a seventh edition of Principles was quickly called for. de Paula dated the Preface to his seventh edition 17 April 1934. It referred to the rapid growth and development of the profession all over the world, and continued:

> ... In fact, this trend has been one of the most notable evolutions in industry and commerce during the past generation. At the same time the outlook of accountants has, in some directions, entirely changed. Perhaps no event throughout the whole period has had so profound an effect on the views of the profession as the Royal Mail Steam Packet case, which undoubtedly will be regarded in the future as an outstanding landmark. That case has completely changed the views of accountants as to their responsibilities in respect of the Profit and Loss Account and as to the creation and utilisation of Secret Reserves.
>
> The preceding edition of this book was revised in the early part of 1933 under the shadow of that all-important case. Later in the same year there was held in London the International Congress of Accounting, which gave the profession an ideal opportunity to take stock of the position as regards this and other vital matters.
>
> In my opinion, the proceedings of that Congress represent a contribution of the first importance in the world of Accountancy. They reveal clearly that the profession is moulding definite principles in regard to the important problems involved in the Royal Mail Steam Packet Company case.
>
> The necessity of bringing out a new edition of this book has given me an opportunity to revise it in the light of these events. I have endeavoured to reflect the latest views of the profession by quoting from and referring to the most important and representative papers given at the recent Congress and elsewhere, thus enabling my readers to obtain a clear view of the opinions held by the leaders of the profession upon the problems that are perplexing all of us.

> In particular I have expanded the text dealing with the Profit and Loss Account, Secret Reserves, Holding Companies, and the treatment of dividends and depreciation.
>
> Wherever I feel my own views to be unorthodox I have called attention to the fact, and have endeavoured clearly to state the traditional view as well as my own ...

From the point of view of the accountancy profession, de Paula's most important contribution during his years at Dunlops was the design and preparation of the company's 1933 accounts which for the first time included consolidated statements. After the lean years of the depression, the Dunlop board in their 1933 accounts were able to report increased profits and to recommend an increased dividend. Following Kylsant, the policy of the Council of the ICAEW had been to look to reform in accounts through the influence of individual members. Their policy was triumphantly vindicated in de Paula's work on the Dunlop accounts for 1933, which had a rapturous reception in the financial press. The Daily Telegraph is worth quoting:

> The 1933 accounts of the Dunlop Rubber Co. will be a joy to its own shareholders and the envy of all others ... Detailed balance sheets, classification according to liquidity, comparative figures and even 'consolidated' statements are now, happily, familiar features of many accounts, though in all these improvements Dunlop has led the way. But no other company has yet had the courage so far to break with tradition as to give what may be called a 'consolidated' profit and loss account, revealing the precise treatment of all subsidiary earnings and segregating all special credits; or to state plainly that all reserves are now disclosed. All these details now appear, and in the most unambiguous terms, with comparative figures in each case. The shareholder can hardly ask for more. It is no doubt too much to hope that all holding companies will speedily follow the Dunlop example, but, now that tradition has once been broken, it is probable that really frank inter-company statements will become more and more common. If so, Dunlop will earn the lasting gratitude of all discerning investors.

The Economist responded similarly, adding:

> The document embodies nearly all that the Economist and other critics of obscurantism have advocated, in season and out of season,for years past, and gives the lie to the familiar assertion that a large holding company cannot afford to go beyond the meagre disclosure laid down by law, for fear of giving away valuable information to its competitors.

The Accountant's review (12 May 1934) included the following:

> ... The shareholders are now presented with a consolidated statement of the assets and liabilities of the company and of its subsidiaries, together with a very clearly compiled statement of profits for the year, showing exactly how the amount available for dividend has been built up. It is

(continued on p.108)

DUNLOP RUBBER CO. LTD.

STATEMENT OF PROFITS FOR THE YEAR 1933

		£	£
I.	The Aggregate Profits of the Dunlop Rubber Co. Ltd. for the year 1933, including its proportion of the profits less losses of all Subsidiary and Sub-subsidiary Companies after providing for Depreciation, &c., but before providing for guaranteed Preference Dividends of Subsidiary Companies amounts to		2,255,973
II.	In addition, the Dunlop Rubber Co.'s proportion of various items which do not represent normal earnings attributable to the current year, amounts to		90,671
III.	Aggregate Total		2,346,644
IV.	From the Results of Subsidiary and Sub-sub-sidiary Companies included above there has been deducted:-		
	(a) The Dunlop Rubber Co.'s proportion of British and Foreign Taxation paid by or provided in the accounts of such companies	229,440	
	(b) The payment on account of the Guaranteed Preference Dividend of Dunlop Plantations, Ltd., for the year to 30th November 1933, made by that Company	41,618	
	(c) The whole of the Guaranteed Preference Dividend of Dunlop Cotton Mills, Ltd., for the year to 31st January 1934 paid by that Company	109,687	
	(d) The whole of the Guaranteed Preference Dividend of Dunlop Co. Rubber (India) Ltd., for the year to 31st December 1933, paid by that Company	13,554	
	(e) The Dunlop Rubber Co.'s proportion of special appropriations and undistributed profits of the year held in reserve	83,421	
			477,720
V.	Balance available to the Dunlop Rubber Co., Ltd., as per that Company's Profit and Loss Account (pages 8 & 9)		1,868,924
VI.	Deduct -		
	(a) Guaranteed Preference Dividends of Sub-sidiary Companies borne by the Dunlop Rubber Co. Ltd.: Balance in respect of Dunlop Plantations Ltd.	70,882	
	(b) Interest on Debentures and Loans	285,176	
			356,058
VII.	Leaving the net Profit as per the Dunlop Rubber Company's Profit and Loss Account (pages 8 & 9)		1,512,866
VIII.	Add Balance brought forward from last year ..		442,208
IX.	Total Available		£1,955,074

DUNLOP RUBBER

BALANCE SHEET AS AT

1932 £		Authorised Shares and Stock £	Issued Shares and Stock £	£
	I. Share Capital -			
	1,000,000 6½% "A" Cum. Pref. Shares of £1 each	1,000,000	1,000,000	
	1,000,000 7% "B" Cum. Pref. Shares of £1 each	1,000,000	1,000,000	
	3,000,000 10% "C" Cum. Pref. Shares of 16s. each	2,400,000	2,400,000	
	£15,600,000 Ord. Stock	15,600,000	7,851,045	12,251,045
12,251,045		£20,000,000		
	II. Surplus and Reserves -			
	(a) Gen. Res. (including balance of Share Prem. A/c) -			
	Bal. at 31st Dec. 1932		1,216,980	
	Less Prem. & Compensations on redemption of 1st Deb. Stock and Costs of new issue		292,137	
			924,843	
	Add Transfer from Profit & Loss Account (page 8)		200,000	
1,216,980			1,124,843	
2,000,000	(b) Special Reserve - against investments in and advances to Subsidiary Cos.		2,000,000	
539,376	(c) Reserves for Contingencies		643,260	
28,338	(d) Reserve for Inter-Co. Profits in Inventory Valuations of Subsid. Cos.		369	
442,208	(e) Surplus, i.e. Profit & Loss A/c Balance after providing for proposed dividends as per Profit & Loss A/c (pages 8 & 9)		578,415	
4,226,902				4,346,887
16,477,947				16,597,932
	III. Debentures and Mortgages secured upon assets of the Company -			
	(a) First Mortgage 5½% Deb. Stock	£5,000,000		
4,366,987	Less Redeemed and cancelled to date	4,715,250	284,750	
	(b) Second Mortgage 6% Debentures	2,000,000		
1,295,290	Less Redeemed and cancelled to date	2,000,000	-	
	(c) 4% Deb. Stock (Authorised £3,500,000)	2,620,000		
	Less uncalled	563,979	2,056,221	
	(d) Mortgage	140,000		
140,000	Less Redeemed to date	140,000	-	2,340,971
5,802,277				
	IV. Amounts owing to Subsidiary and Associated Companies (Less Dividends since declared) -			
	(a) Subsidiary Companies	1,473,543		
	Less Co.'s own Deb. Stock included therein	11,028		
1,601,423		1,462,515		
50,824	(b) Associated Companies	51,144	1,513,659	
1,652,247				

31ST DECEMBER 1933

1932 £			£	£
	I. Fixed Assets at Cost, less Realisations and Depreciation -			
1,948,067	(a) Freehold Land and Buildings		1,884,801	
424,843	(b) Leasehold Premises		401,043	
1,295,222	(c) Plant, Machinery, Tools & Moulds		1,164,050	
151,681	(d) Furniture, Fittings and Fixtures		145,187	
8,979	(e) Cars and Delivery Vans		8,965	
640,564	(f) Patents, Trade Marks, Licences and Royalty Agreements as valued by the Directors at 31st Dec. 1926, plus additions at cost, less amounts written off		640,564	
4,469,356				4,244,610
	II. Investments and Advances at Cost, less amounts written off and Reserves -			
	Subsidiary Companies:			
4,960,847	(a) Shares		4,932,478	
196,593	(b) Debentures		196,593	
7,159,116	(c) Advances and Current Accounts (including dividends since declared)		6,686,425	
12,316,556	(In respect of this amount an allocation of £2,000,000 to Special Reserve was made in 1931, as per contra)		11,815,496	
	Associated Companies:			
930,626	(d) Shares		977,087	
179,363	(e) Advances and Current Accounts (including dividends since declared)		114,225	
	Sundry Investments:			
	(f) In hands of Trustees for Deb. Holders:-			
73,823	British Governm't Securities at Cost (Market Value at 31st Dec. 1933, £80,202)	£73,823		
3,083	Cash	15,442	89,265	
19,261	(g) Trade Investments		18,323	13,014,396
13,522,712				
	III. Current Assets -			
1,817,322	(a) Inventories of finished and unfinished goods, raw materials and stores, &c., at or below cost as certified by the Company's officials		1,868,590	
834,944	(b) Sundry Debtors, less Reserves		817,775	
22,400	(c) Leasehold Redemption Policy		26,133	
55,214	(d) Bills Receivable		85,639	
977,332	(e) British Government Securities at Cost (Market Value at 31st Dec. 1933 £7,594)		7,503	
281,691	(f) Other Securities		19,097	
11,061	(g) Accrued Interest		5,597	
3,245,225	(h) Bank Balances, Deposits, Cash in Hand and in Transit		2,097,232	
18,797	(i) Deferred Charges		26,477	4,954,143
7,263,986				

Continued overleaf

1932		1933	
	V. Current Liabilities and Provisions -		
	(a) Sundry Creditors, including accrued		
477,427	Deb. and Mortgage Interest	545,010	
	(b) Proposed Dividends -		
	Pref. Divs. for half year to 31st Dec.		
140,625	1933 less Income Tax	145,312	
	Ord. Div. for the year to 31st Dec.		
235,531	1933, less Income Tax	486,765	
470,000	(c) Taxation Reserve	583,500	
			1,760,587
1,323,583			
£25,256,054			£22,213,149

REPORT OF THE AUDITORS TO THE MEMBERS OF THE DUNLOP RUBBER CO., LTD.

In accordance with the provisions of Section 134, subsection (I), of the Companies Act, 1929, we report as follows:-

We have audited the above Balance Sheet with the Books of the Company in which have been incorporated the Returns from Branches certified by Local Auditors or the Branch Officials, and we have obtained all the information and explanations we have required. In our opinion such Balance Sheet is properly drawn up so as to exhibit a true and correct view of the state of the Company's affairs according to the best of our information and the explanations given to us and as shown by the Books of the Company and the said Returns. - London, 28th April 1934.

STOKES BROS. & PIM,
WHINNEY, SMITH & WHINNEY,
Auditors, Chartered Accountants.

NOTE. - The Company has guaranteed the Preference Shares of Dunlop Cotton Mills Ltd., Dunlop Plantations, Ltd., and Dunlop Rubber Co. (India) Ltd., as regards Capital, Premium and Dividends, and is also contingently liable in respect of the guarantee of Bank advances to certain Subsidiary Companies.

ERIC GEDDES, Chairman.
J. GEORGE BEHARRELL, Managing Director.
C. TENNYSON, Secretary.

£25,256,054	£22,213,149

DUNLOP RUBBER

PROFIT AND LOSS ACCOUNT FOR THE

Dr.

1932 £				£
361,304	I.	To Depreciation, &c.		355,932
200,000	II.	" Obsolescence Reserve		-
8,000	III.	" Directors' Fees		8,000
1,353,064	IV.	" Balance carried down		1,868,924
1,922,368				£2,232,856
	V.	To Guaranteed Preference Dividends -		
106,884		(a) Part in respect of Dunlop Plantations Ltd.	£70,882	
13,500		(b) The whole in respect of Dunlop Rubber Co. (India) Ltd.	-	70,882
120,384				
372,603	VI.	" Interest on Debentures and Loans		285,176
860,077	VII.	" Net Profit carried down		1,512,866
1,353,064				£1,868,924
292,947	VIII.	To Transfer to Taxation Reserve		403,957
-	IX.	" Transfer to General Reserve		200,000
	X.	" Preference Dividends -		
140,625		(a) Half year to 30th June 1933 (already paid) less Income Tax at 5s. in the £	£140,625	
140,625		(b) Proposed for the half year to 31st Dec. 1933, less Income Tax at 4s.6d. in the £	145,312	285,937
	XI.	" Ordinary Dividend -		
235,531		Proposed for the year to 31st December 1933, less Inoome Tax at 4s.6d. in the £		486,765
442,208	XII.	" Balance carried forward as per Balance Sheet		578,415
£1,251,936				£1,955,074

CO. LTD.

YEAR ENDED 31ST DECEMBER 1933

1932 £		Cr. £
1,922,368	I. By Profit on Trading, Interest, Dividends on Investments, including those received from or since declared by Subsidiary and Associated Companies, and Miscellaneous Receipts	2,215,890
-	II. " Repayment by Dunlop Rubber Co. (India) Ltd., on account of Guaranteed Preference Dividends paid by the Dunlop Rubber Co., Ltd., in previous years	16,966
1,922,368		£2,232,856
1,353,064	III. By Balance brought down	1,868,924
1,353,064		£1,868,924
860,077	IV. By Net Profit brought down	1,512,866
391,859	" Balance brought forward from 1932	442,208
£1,251,936		£1,955,074

NOTE. - The Profits of Subsidiary Companies are included in the profits of this Company to the extent of the dividends declared in respect of the year 1933.

In the case of those Subsidiary Companies which have sustained losses this Company's proportion thereof has been provided for out of the profits as above set forth with the exception of certain losses of a capital nature which have been charged against the Reserve for Contingencies.

In the accounts of the Subsidiary Companies these losses have been either carried forward or provided for out of undistributed profits of those Companies.

CONSOLIDATED STATEMENT OF ASSETS AND

DUNLOP RUBBER CO., LTD.

Incorporating the figures of the audited Balance Sheets (after elimination
Subsidiary and sub-Subsidiary Companies in which the Dunlop Rubber Co.,
Ordinary Shares or Stock of those
voting

		£	£
I. Issued Share Capital of the Dunlop Rubber Co., Ltd.-			
1,000,000 6½% "A" Cum. Pref. Shares of £1 each, fully paid		1,000,000	
1,000,000 7% "B" Cum. Pref. Shares of £1 each, fully paid		1,000,000	
3,000,000 10% "C" Cum. Pref. Shares of 16s each, fully paid		2,400,000	
£7,851,045 6s.8d. Ordinary Stock		7,851,045	12,251,045
II. Surplus and Reserves -			
(a) General Reserves		1,309,668	
(b) Special Reserve in the accounts of the Dunlop Rubber Co., Ltd., in respect of Subsidiary Companies		2,000,000	
(c) Reserves for Contingencies		643,260	
(d) Surplus, i.e. Profit and Loss Account Credit Balances		661,943	4,614,871
			16,865,916
III. Interest of outside Shareholders -			
Pref. and Ord. Share Capital of Subsidiaries held by Outside Shareholders, after taking into account their proportion of General Reserves and Undistributed Profits or Losses attributable thereto			6,153,496
IV. Debentures, Mortgages and Loans -			
(a) Dunlop Rubber Co., Ltd., Deb. Stock	£2,340,971		
Less Held by Subsid. Co.	11,028	2,329,943	
(b) Loans		785,941	
(c) Mortgages		10,000	3,125,884
V. Current Liabilities and Provisions -			
(a) Sundry Creditors and Accrued Charges		1,647,382	
(b) Amounts owing to Associated Cos.		51,144	
(c) Taxation Reserves		864,439	
(d) Proposed Dividends -			
Dunlop Rubber Co., Ltd., Dividends		632,077	
Divs. of Subsidiaries to Outside Shareholders		74,632	3,269,674
VI. Suspense Account for transactions with Subsidiary Cos. between the dates of their Balance Sheets and 31st Dec. 1933			1,284
VII. Exchange Suspense Accounts, being amounts Reserved for Unrealised Exchange Differences			4,371
			£29,420,625

We have examined the above Consolidated Statement of Assets and Liabilities with the
with the Balance Sheets of the Subsidiary and Sub-subsidiary Companies, as audited by their
are at dates other than 31st December 1933, and the adjustments consequent thereon have been
the said Balance Sheets, after giving effect to necessary adjustments in respect of Foreign
the Companies at 31st December 1933. - London, 28th April 1934.

AND SUBSIDIARY COMPANIES

of inter-company balances) of the Dunlop Rubber Co., Ltd. and all
Ltd. and any of its Subsidiaries hold over 50 per cent. of the
companies or over 50 per cent. of the
control.

	£	£
I. Fixed Assets, at cost less realisations and provisions for depreciation and obsolescence -		
(a) Land, Factory, and other Buildings, Cotton Mills, Plant, Tools, Furniture, Cars, &c.	10,716,376	
(b) Dunlop Plantations, Ltd., Estates, Buildings, Plant, &c.	4,207,677	
(c) Patents, Trade Marks, Licences, &c.	640,564	15,564,617
II. Investments, at Cost less amounts written off -		
(a) Investments in Associated Companies	977,087	
(b) British Government Securities at Cost, and Cash in hands of Trustees for Debenture Holders	89,265	
(c) Trade and Sundry Investments	129,285	1,195,637
III. Current Assets -		
(a) Inventories at or below cost	5,278,893	
(b) Sundry Debtors, Bills Receivable, &c., less Reserves	2,995,766	
(c) Amounts owing by Associated Cos.	114,225	
(d) British and Canadian Government Securities (market value at 31st Dec. 1933 £134,544)	134,021	
(e) Other Securities	54,675	
(f) Bank Balances and Cash	2,668,341	
(g) Deferred Charges	90,787	11,336,708
IV. Goodwill Accounts, including the difference between the values at which inter-company holdings of shares are taken as assets into the Balance Sheets and their Par Values, less undistributed profits at the date of the acquisition of such shares		1,323,663
		£29,420,625

ERIC GEDDES, Chairman.
J. GEORGE BEHARRELL, Managing Director.
C. TENNYSON, Secretary.

Balance Sheet of the Dunlop Rubber Co., Ltd., at 31st December 1933, as audited by us, and
respective auditors. In the case of certain Subsidiary Companies, the Balance Sheets
made. In our opinion, the statement set forth above has been correctly compiled from
Exchange, so as to exhibit a true and correct view of the consolidated position of

STOKES BROS. & PYM,
WHINNEY, SMITH & WHINNEY,
Chartered Accountants.

perhaps worthy of note that the consolidated statement has been reported on by the auditors to the effect that it has been 'correctly compiled from the balance sheets after giving effect to necessary adjustments in respect of foreign exchange, so as to exhibit a true and correct view of the consolidated position of the companies.' With regard to the legal balance sheet of the company, we should like to remark that we think it is an excellent model. The grouping is good, and the headings are logically arranged so that even the inexpert shareholder may get a clear idea of the financial situation. Not least amongst the merits of this publication, in our view, is that it has boldly adopted the practice of eliminating shillings and pence from the figures. Much space is thereby saved, and a greater sense of proportion is achieved. We wish that the practice were more general. The name of Mr. F.R.M. de Paula does not appear on the accounts, but most Chartered Accountants will recognise his influence on the publication. We should like to congratulate Mr. de Paula and all those associated with him in the financial management of the company on a very excellent production, which is likely to rank as a model.

In its 'Finance and Commerce' section, in the same issue, The Accountant noted, inter alia:

> This is also the first occasion for the issue of a Consolidated Statement of the Assets and Liabilities of the Dunlop and subsidiary companies. In this we must certainly commend the directors for including sub-subsidiary companies, the point of consolidation being where the Dunlop Company owns 50 per cent of the ordinary capital or voting control of the subsidiaries or sub-subsidiaries. This practice of stating the point of consolidation should be generally adopted. The essential aim in this account has been to make the fullest disclosure that is possible. This has resulted even in the disclosure of a reserve for obsolescence previously deducted from 'Shares in Subsidiaries', by transferring it to the reserve for contingencies. Such complete frankness may not find approval in some quarters, but it is a policy which we feel can only produce good. Its adoption by such an important concern as the Dunlop Company cuts the ground completely from under those arguments which inevitably end with 'not in the interests of the company'. The strength of the position as shown by the combined statement is immense, current assets representing 38½ per cent of the capital employed and showing a surplus over current liabilities of £8 million. The capital structure is interesting. Debentures, mortgages and loans represent only £3,125,884 out of a total of £29,420,625. In the facility with which these facts can be read off from the accounts is a practical example of the advantages of a suitable grouping of balance sheet items. May we presume that comparative figures will be given next year in the Consolidated Accounts.

de Paula put together a lecture on the 1933 Dunlop accounts ('The Form of Presentation of the Accounts of Holding Companies' reprinted in Developments in Accounting and elsewhere) which he delivered to CA Students' Societies of London and Birmingham and also to the Sussex Branch of the South Eastern CA Students' Society in November 1934. He made a tremendous impression on his audiences. Nevertheless, inertia in the business world and in the profession was such that general adoption of consolidated statements was delayed into the 1940s, despite a ruling by the Council of the London Stock Exchange in March 1939 requiring all holding companies seeking a new quotation to publish consolidated accounts.

The Dunlop Company's reputation benefited, and, to use a term unfamiliar in 1934, its 'image' was considerably enhanced by the much lauded 1933 accounts. Nevertheless, from the Company's point of view, Frederic de Paula's main contribution lay in his work in developing budgetary control within the Company and in financial planning and control generally. de Paula gave a number of lectures in these areas (reproduced in Developments in Accounting). They included 'The Role of Finance and Accountancy in the Management of large Business Combines' presented to the British Association for the Advancement of Science in 1933; 'The Principles and Practice of Budgeting in Modern Business', delivered to CA Students' Societies in 1936 (with Lord Plender in the chair at the London lecture); 'The Valuation of Stock-in-Trade or Inventories' presented to the CASSL in February 1937; and 'Financial Planning: Insuring for Future Profits', a public lecture given at the Regent Street Polytechnic in 1939. In 1939, also, de Paula gave a further lecture on 'The Form of Presentation of the Accounts of Holding Companies' in an address to the Birmingham and District Society of Chartered Accountants.

The Second World War

When war became imminent, de Paula was lent by Dunlops in June 1939 to the War Office, where he held the appointment of Deputy Director-General of Progress and Statistics, and where he worked until he was recalled to Dunlops in March 1940. In 1940 and 1941, he had a long period of serious illness, and at the end of 1941 retired from the Dunlop Company, going as Vice-Chairman and Joint Managing Director to Harding, Tilton and Hartley Ltd. (later to be known as the British Van Heusen Co.). de Paula became chairman of that Company, and served also on the boards of other important companies.

In 1942, de Paula presented a paper on 'Government Contract Cost Investigations' to the London Members of the ICAEW, opening his talk with an outline of the negotiations lately completed between the Federation of British Industries and the Treasury which had resulted in an agreed statement of guidance. de Paula had been chairman of the sub-committee of the F.B.I. which had dealt with the matter (Developments in Accounting, pp.245-261).

The ICAEW's Taxation and Financial Relations Committee and the Recommendations on Accounting Principles

As the 1930s had drawn to a close, there had been evidence among members of the ICAEW of some uneasiness with regard to the membership and role of the Council. In 1941, there was a move to open the Council to younger members, and particularly to members directly employed in industry and commerce whose numbers had been steadily growing for well over a decade. One idea canvassed at the time was, in due course, to enable returning servicemen to participate more fully. The Council was ready to respond to such pressures in 1942, and set up in that year a Taxation and Financial Relations Committee, with the main intention that it should serve as an instrument to promote liaison on business and financial problems with provincial members, and especially between members in practice and in industry. Regional sub-committees were established in the District Societies. The move was timely for in the autumn of 1942 the ICAEW and the Society of Incorporated Accountants and Auditors were both under attack in papers like The Economist for being out of touch with their members in industry.

The ICAEW's T and FR Committee (forerunner of the present Technical Advisory Committee) met for the first time in July 1942: H.M. Barton (later Sir Harold, and President of the ICAEW 1944-1945) was elected Chairman, and Frederic de Paula Vice-Chairman. At the July meeting it was unanimously agreed that Stanley W. Rowland (a partner in Dicksee's firm since 1924 and for many years Lecturer in Accounting at LSE) should be approached to act as Secretary of the Committee. At its second meeting, in August 1942, the T and FR Committee set up a General Advisory Sub-Committee '... to consider, *inter alia*, general questions of accounting principles and procedure ...'. The Council's first Recommendations on Accounting Principles (nos. I and II, dealing respectively with tax reserve certificates and war damage contributions, premiums and claims) were published on 12 December 1942. Three more Recommendations (dealing with the treatment of taxation - including special war-time taxation - in accounts, the treatment in accounts of income tax deductible from dividends payable and annual charges, and the inclusion in accounts of proposed profit appropriations) were published on 13 March 1943.

Harold Barton resigned as Chairman of the T and FR Committee on 18 March 1943, and was replaced by Kenneth Arthur Layton-Bennett. In Layton-Bennett's absence at the next meeting (his health was deteriorating) de Paula as Vice-Chairman took the Chair, and he chaired the subsequent meetings until elected to the Chairmanship of the T and FR Committee on a regular basis on 18 November 1943. Publication of the important Recommendations on reserves and provisions (no. VI) and on the disclosure of the financial position and results of subsidiary companies in the accounts of holding companies (no. VII) took place on 23 October 1943 and 12 February 1944. No. VIII, on the form of the balance sheet and profit and loss account, followed on 15 July 1944. Recommendations IX and X (on the depreciation of fixed assets and the valuation of stock-in-trade) appeared in January and June 1945.

Recommendation VI (reserves and provisions) was unequivocally in favour of the disclosure of all reserves in the balance sheet. For provisions, the Recommendation was that 'Only in circumstances where disclosure of the amount of a particular provision would clearly be detrimental to the interests of a company should it be included under another heading, for example "Creditors"; the fact that such heading includes "Provisions" should then be indicated in the narrative.' The Recommendation concluded:

> Subject [as above] in regard to provisions the disclosure of which would be detrimental to the interests of a company, where reserves and provisions are created or increased, the amounts involved, if material, and the sources from which they have been created or increased, should be disclosed in the accounts. In all cases the utilisation of reserves, and of provisions proved to have been redundant, should be disclosed in the accounts.

This Recommendation of October 1943 sounded the death knell of the secret or undisclosed reserve. The principles it incorporated were to be included in the 1947/48 legislation as a main plank in the new structure of requirements for disclosure. It is interesting to note that the subjects of the Recommendations (nos. VI to X) published between October 1943 and June 1945 followed exactly the list of subjects identified by de Paula in his 1933 Preface to Principles of Auditing (except that the Recommendations did not yet deal with forward contracts) as those on which, in 1933, 'the profession [had] not made up its mind' and with regard to which 'some form of uniform practice should be adopted by the profession ...' or which should at least be the subject of 'accepted and established principles'.

Frederic de Paula retired from the Chairmanship of the T and FR Committee in 1945. He was under heavy pressure and dividing his time between Taunton (Harding, Tilton & Hartley Ltd.) and London. He had a number of important directorships, and the shadow of his illness of 1940/41 still lay upon him.

The first non-practising member of the Council

In December 1943, Frederic de Paula had been elected to the Council of the ICAEW as its first non-practising member. The move created considerable interest in the financial press. Inside the profession, The Accountant's Weekly Note of 11 December 1943 was indicative of widely shared views:

> At its meeting held on 1st December, which is reported in another part of this issue, the Council of the Institute and Mr. F.R.M. de Paula together made history. Through the election of Mr. de Paula to a seat on the Council, the Institute now has for the first time in the 63 years of its existence a direct representative of the large and growing number of members engaged in industry. In addition to the recognition of Mr. de Paula's individual wisdom and experience, it is a general indication that the Council Chamber is not a closed room to those who, while not publicly practising the profession of accountancy, have an increasingly valuable contribution to make to the corporate life of the parent body, and it may well be regarded as a very important first step towards closing a gap which was a weakness in the ranks of the profession. There will be general satisfaction that the choice has fallen upon one who has had so distinguished a career and whose opinions are so widely respected.

Evidence to the Cohen Committee (1943-45)

Frederic de Paula took the rather unusual step of submitting a personal Memorandum of Evidence to the Cohen Committee on Company Law Amendment which had been appointed in June 1943 to consider amendments to the 1929 Companies Act. He reprinted his Memorandum in 1948 in Developments in Accounting. It ran to about 7,000 words and covered a wide range of matters, giving primacy to the issue of secret reserves (looking to '... full disclosure of all reserves and their utilisation ...') and much weight to financial disclosure by holding companies through consolidated statements ('... A reasonably clear view of the financial position and trading results of a group of companies can, in my view, be obtained only by the preparation of a consolidated balance sheet together with a consolidated statement of earnings ...').

de Paula's Memorandum was dated 14 September 1943, and we may presume that he prepared it during the summer of that year while the draft Recommendations VI and VII (on reserves and provisions, and on the disclosure of the financial position and results of subsidiary companies in the accounts of holding companies) were in their late stages and before the Council of the ICAEW for final acceptance. In the end, Recommendation VI (published on 23 October 1943) must have met de Paula's requirements as a statement of 'best practice', and he must have been very satisfied, similarly, with Recommendation VII despite its listing three methods of disclosure, namely:

(1) To submit copies of the accounts of each of the subsidiary undertakings ...

(2) To submit statements of the consolidated assets and liabilities and of the aggregate earnings of the subsidiary undertakings as distinct from those of the holding company ...

(3) To submit a consolidated balance sheet and a consolidated profit and loss account of the holding company and of its subsidiary undertakings treated as one group ...

because the Recommendation (when it was published on 12 February 1944) said of Methods (1) and (2) that 'The first and second methods are suitable only in special cases' and of Method (3), 'This method is the most suitable for general application'.

The ICAEW's own Memorandum of Evidence to the Cohen Committee was dated December 1943, and was less positive in its recommendations in favour of consolidated statements than was de Paula in his Memorandum, or, indeed, than was Recommendation VII itself by the time it was published. The Cohen Committee's 1945 Report, which formed the basis for the 1947/48 legislation, followed de Paula and Recommendation VII. The ICAEW's representatives (Sir Harold Howitt, President of the ICAEW in 1945-46, and Thomas Buston Robson, President in 1952-53 and later Sir Thomas) gave oral evidence to the Cohen Committee on 25 February 1944. Frederic de Paula gave oral evidence to the Committee on 19 May 1944.

<u>Refresher courses for returned servicemen</u>

In 1942, de Paula canvassed the idea amongst accountants serving in the Forces, and in 1943 was among the first to raise the proposal that when the war ended the ICAEW might provide 'Refresher Courses' in some suitable form for young qualified men returning from war service. Later in 1943, and in 1944, the ICAEW was seeking advice and help to this end from District Societies and public and private sector educational institutions, considering ways in which the work might be done, and asking members to assist, especially in preparing notes under a range of headings which could be published and form the basis for such courses or for use by discussion groups.

de Paula's initial proposal had been that an ideal form of refresher course would be residential (for up to four weeks) involving a group of 25 to 30 returned servicemen and held either in a residential centre to be specially established in a country location or possibly in one of the Oxford or Cambridge Colleges during vacation. The suggestion was that prominent members of the profession should visit the course to introduce topics of importance and to take part in discussions, getting to know the course-members and spending a day and a night with the course.

The ICAEW pursued the proposal for the establishment of a residential centre, but the difficulties involved at that time eventually proved insuperable. Residential courses were held, however, in Colleges from 1945 and they proved immensely successful. de Paula was Director of Studies at the first course at Emmanuel College, Cambridge in August and September 1945. Stanley Rowland was among the visiting speakers. In the spring of 1946,courses were held at three Cambridge Colleges (Downing, Pembroke, and Jesus) and at The Queens College, Oxford. All were of three weeks' duration. de Paula was again Director of Studies for the first week of the Pembroke course and the last week of the course at Jesus. Members of the Taxation and Financial Relations Committee were prominent among the visiting speakers. In the summer of 1946, five more courses were held in Oxford and Cambridge, with de Paula and Rowland again Directors of Studies. These courses were the precursors of the ICAEW's Summer Schools.

Altogether, according to the President's Address at the 1947 Annual Meeting of the ICAEW (The Accountant, 17 May 1947, p.280) ten refresher courses were held in Oxford or Cambridge Colleges and, in addition, the District Societies, including London, arranged afternoon or evening lectures and discussion groups for over 1,000 members returned from war service.

After a short illness, Stanley Rowland died on 31 October 1946 when he was still comparatively young. He had willingly shouldered a heavy extra burden in his work for the T and FR Committee and the Refresher courses. He had for years had a reputation for hard work, and through the war years had continually accepted additional responsibilities. He was sadly missed.

Rising price levels

Frederic de Paula gave a wide-ranging lecture in March 1943 (reprinted in The Accountant of 5 May 1943 and in Developments in Accounting) on 'The Future of the Accountancy Profession'. In it, he included the following paragraph:

> A most important problem that may arise after the war is whether the items in balance sheets will require re-valuation if the price level moves by reason of inflation. This vital problem urgently requires thinking out for the benefit of industry and our profession.

Not surprisingly, de Paula was not able in 1943 and in the years that followed to 'think out' any satisfactory solution to this problem. Indeed, it is apparent from part of his 1944 evidence to the Cohen Committee that his grasp of value concepts for balance sheet assets was not always strong.

Nevertheless, he recognised a major problem area and returned to the issue more than once. He spoke in May 1948 to a joint meeting of the professional accountancy bodies in Brighton. There he did not clearly disentangle the consequences of a change in general price levels from the consequences of changes in the prices of specific assets (buildings, plant, stock) but talked of a general replacement value approach to income and asset values, linking this with what he termed 'the view of the economists' that 'the purpose of an industrial undertaking should be to preserve intact for all time the original production capacity'. On this basis, the economists argued, in times of rising prices, that the cost of the increased amount of money capital required 'to replace fixed assets and augment working capital ... should be provided for ... out of revenue'.

As de Paula saw it, and, indeed, as many economists certainly saw it at the time:

> The reason why the economists are pressing this matter ... is that they wish to measure accurately the national income and the national investment in durable goods. If, therefore, accounts were all prepared on the foregoing basis, they contend that their published accounts would enable these vital national statistics to be compiled.

de Paula continued:

> The important matter we have to consider is whether it is practicable and correct to prepare accounts on this basis and whether published accounts can serve the purpose desired by the economists.

de Paula foresaw many practical difficulties, and in particular the issue as to what purpose(s) accounts were intended to serve and whether they could usefully be prepared on a 'multi-purpose basis'. He saw a fundamental question in 'whether provisions for increases in the capital requirements of a company represent a charge against earnings or an appropriation', adding, '... if the latter it is obviously a matter of financial policy with which the auditor is not concerned'.

This was, in fact, his conclusion, though he stressed that he put it forward very hesitantly. He came down in favour of the 'financial policy' argument, stressing that all prudent boards of directors ploughed back profits. But he emphasised the importance of '/making/ clear what has been done and what is the true position of affairs ... An ideal would be for the board to make an estimate and disclose the total extra capital required and also state the aggregate amount that had been set aside for this contingency ...'

de Paula spoke again on 'The Effects of the Price Level on Accounting' in a lecture to the CASS of Edinburgh in October 1952, after the ICAEW's Recommendation XII of January 1949 (rising price levels in relation to accounts) and Recommendation XV of May 1952 (accounting in relation to changes in the purchasing power of money) had both appeared, and after the subject had had some debate at the 1952 International Congress on Accounting in London. However, he did not take significantly further his arguments and conclusions of 1948, except to recognise the possibilities of publishing one or more supplementary statements along with the legal accounts of companies.

The Carr-Saunders Report on Education for Commerce

In June 1946, the then Minister of Education (the Rt. Hon. Ellen Wilkinson) set up a Committee on Education for Commerce with the following terms of reference:

> To consider the provision which should be made for education for commerce and for the professions relating to it, and the respective contributions to be made thereto by universities and by colleges and departments of commerce in England and Wales.

Sir Alexander M. Carr-Saunders, Director of the London School of Economics since 1937, and co-author of an important book on the professions, was appointed Chairman. A distinguished group of educationists and others including Sir Arnold Plant, Sir Ernest Cassel Professor of Commerce at LSE, and Professor J.G. Smith,

OBE of the Faculty of Commerce, Birmingham University, was brought together on the Committee. Frederic de Paula was asked to serve as a member and agreed to do so.

In 1946, de Paula was at the zenith of his career in terms of his place in the profession and the regard in which he was held. He had been a member of the Council of the Institute for three years and was, of course, himself a former Sir Ernest Cassel Professor at LSE, having resigned his Chair in Accountancy and Business Methods at the end of 1929. He was a natural choice for membership of the Committee.

The Carr-Saunders Committee reported in the autumn of 1949. The Rt. Hon. George Tomlinson, the then Minister of Education, noted in a foreword to the Report that the enquiry had 'been exacting ... because it was concerned with a very wide field which had never before been fully surveyed'. This is not the place to consider the content of the Report save in so far as it affected de Paula's relations with the Council of the ICAEW. Sir Harold Howitt in his History of the Institute of Chartered Accountants in England and Wales: 1870-1965 deals with it at pp.109-110 and 189-190. Professor David Solomons deals with it in greater detail in Prospectus for a Profession, a Report of the Long Range Enquiry into Education and Training for the Accountancy Profession which he wrote with T.M. Berridge for the Advisory Board of Accountancy Education in 1974 (pp.22-26).

Because of the generality of their terms of reference, and because the Committee were anxious not to get into difficulties in attempting to distinguish between education for commerce, and education for particular professions operating in the commercial field, they chose a very wide definition of the word 'profession' in interpreting their terms of reference, thus:

> ... we understand by the word 'profession' in our terms of reference any body of persons, using a common technique, however meagre in content and however little related to fundamental study, who form an association one purpose of which is to test competence in the technique by means of examinations.

As David Solomons was to observe in Prospectus for a Profession (p.23) this was not a definition 'calculated to win friends for the Committee', yet they had been understandably anxious not to have to decide 'where to draw the line between vocations which can properly be called professions in the traditional sense, and those which cannot be so denominated' (Report, Chap. 1).

Moreover, the Carr-Saunders Committee's Report included the following (amongst other things) in its Summary and Recommendations under a heading 'Professional Examinations':

> Professional associations in the field of commercial education should be invited to give consideration to the following proposals of this committee:-
>
> > At the stage of the intermediate examination only general commercial subjects should be prescribed, vocational training being introduced only at the final stage.
> >
> > Entry upon vocational training at too early an age should be discouraged and recruits to the professions under the age of eighteen should be advised to take national certificate courses. Unnecessary variation in syllabuses in common subjects should be eliminated.
>
> Courses in technical colleges for professional examinations should be extensively developed. Day-time facilities for training should be available, and day courses on the part-time or the 'sandwich' principle, giving preparation for the intermediate and final examinations of the main professional bodies and associations, should be organised on a regional basis.

Solomons comments (p.24):

> The Committee's conclusions were dramatically opposed to the views presented to it in evidence by the Institute's spokesmen and the Institutute's reaction to the report, embodied in a 50-page report by the Council, can fairly be described as explosive.

The Council's report was dated March 1951, though it had originally been drafted at least a year earlier, but had not been issued:

> as it was not then known what action, if any, the Minister of Education would take after consideration of the report of the Carr-Saunders Committee. It is now evident that the Minister is anxious to implement some of the recommendations of the Carr-Saunders Committee and it has therefore become important that the views of the Council should be available to everyone who may be concerned.

Earlier the Council's Report had noted:

> All evidence given on behalf of the Institute was contrary to the recommendations now made by the Carr-Saunders Committee, although the committee's report gives no hint of that fact.
>
> It should be mentioned that although Mr. F.R.M. de Paula, C.B.E., F.C.A., was a member of the Carr-Saunders Committee and was at that time a member of the Council of the Institute, his appointment to the Carr-Saunders Committee was a personal one and not in any way as a representative or nominee of the Council. Nor do the views expressed in the report which he signed agree with those of the Council.

> The present report by the Council has been prepared to show why the Council is unable to support any move which may be made with the object of applying the recommendations of the Carr-Saunders Committee to the method of qualifying for membership of the Institute.

The first section of the report concluded:

> The Council would offer the strongest opposition to the disintegration of the Institute's examinations or the system of training under articles. Whatever merits the recommendations of the Carr-Saunders Committee may have in relation to other occupations - a matter with which the Council of the Institute is not concerned - the Council considers that they can have no place in the education and training for membership of the Institute.

Clearly, Council members were gravely concerned and seriously displeased with de Paula, though within a few years they were to appoint their own Committee on Education and Training (the Parker Committee, 1958). When that Committee's Report was published in 1961, its general tenor appeared to be firmly in favour of the status quo. It did however recommend a reduction in the period of articles to four years for candidates who had both remained at school until the age of 17½ and obtained passes in two subjects at Advanced Level, and it left the door open for various further reviews and enquiries, including the feasibility of arranging for the provision of full-time courses by local educational bodies to be given in the periods before the intermediate and final examinations. In the event, developments in education and training for ICAEW after 1961 proceeded faster than a reading of the Parker Report might have implied and in 1966 the Council decided to introduce 9 months' (Foundation) courses on a voluntary basis 'as a first step towards a new approach to education and training' recognising that short-term practical considerations made it necessary in the first instance for the period of the course to be within articles. These 9 months' courses were the forerunners of the present Foundation Courses provided in Polytechnics and some major Colleges for non-graduates wishing to enter training contracts. From 1971, entry requirements for trainees were raised to a two 'A' Level standard, and thereafter the acceptance of applications for training contracts by school-leavers with 'O' Level qualifications alone was steadily reduced.

de Paula was much affected by the strength of the Council's disagreement with the Carr-Saunders Committee's Report, which it seems clear that he had not adequately foreseen. Already, in 1947, his load of other work and the general state of his health had inclined him to resign from the Council of the ICAEW, though he had been dissuaded. At the end of 1949, however, he tendered his resignation on grounds of health and other commitments and in January 1950 it was accepted. It seemed a sad end to an association he had greatly valued but he retained many friends on the Council and on Council Committees.

Closing years

In 1950 also, Frederic de Paula resigned from the Taxation Committee of the Federation of British Industries, of which he had been a member since 1932 and Chairman since 1941. He was appointed CBE in the Civil List in the New Year Honours of 1951, in part following his work on a Government Committee appointed to review the organisation and administrative methods of the Inland Revenue Department. (His OBE was in the Military List and by custom was retained.) In 1951 also, he brought out the eleventh edition of Principles of Auditing. In 1952, at the Sixth International Congress on Accounting, held in London, de Paula was chosen to present the first paper in the section on 'The Accountant in Industry'. Rehabilitation was by then well advanced.

No argument is needed to establish that de Paula was a man of wide-ranging interests and achievements. Perhaps we cannot end this chapter better than by quoting from an obituary note written in 1954 by F.M. Rees, MC, FCA, Chief Accountant of Unilever and Lever Bros. Ltd., and an old friend and colleague:

> [Frederic de Paula] had an exceptional clarity and simplicity of expression in his numerous publications and lectures and a lively sense of humour, coupled with a great strength of character in adhering to his opinions which at times were in advance of his day. Many members now in practice must look back with appreciation to his initiative and endless trouble in establishing and running the residential courses at the universities after the last War which will always be remembered as the forerunners of the annual Summer Courses which are now so popular.
>
> Many of us have lost a personal friend, but in mourning our loss we must be thankful that he fulfilled what I know was his ambition - to promote the welfare of our students and generally to raise the prestige of the Institute and of its members in practice and in industry and commerce.